PLANT PEACE

CHEYANNE HOLLIDAY

W0010962

WelcomeHohm.org

Dedicated to *you, beloved.*

CONTENTS

NOTE TO READER

Hello love. I would first like to thank you for picking up this book. It is the culmination of years of activism, investigations, scientific research and spiritual growth. Throughout these pages we will be exploring the reality of animal agriculture, the problems that have arisen as a result of humanities actions and the solutions we have available at hand. Here, I will share my personal experiences with these industries and the dreams I have for a new, peaceful world. I will also be offering my favorite plant-based recipes, many of which come directly from the restaurant I previously owned. As you read this, I encourage you to ponder creative solutions of your own, and I challenge you to bring these ideas to life. I also ask that you contemplate the following questions as we journey through this book together:

How do you value life?

What does your life mean to you?

How do you determine the value of life?

Introduction

Plant began as a seedling of an idea; planted, watered and nourished by the wonderful people around me. I moved to Fairfield, Iowa to attend Maharishi University of Management (now Maharishi International University) fresh outta high school. I was young, ambitious, excited and halfway across the country from everything I had ever known. It was the definition of "out of my comfort zone."

I came to school ready to make an impact. Back home, I had established an animal rights group called PEACE: Promoting Equality, Acceptance & Compassion Everywhere. I had organizers back home that intended to continue holding events, as I was to start a new branch here in Iowa. I quickly learned that the weekly street activism I was used to wouldn't be the most applicable in my new home. This was mostly because I felt afraid. I was used to being surrounded and supported by experienced vegan activists. Now, I was deep in the heart of animal agriculture and as far as I could tell, I was the only one with any training in this arena.

I quickly made friends, many of whom were vegan or became vegan in the following weeks. I organized an event with some activists from out of town and it was fairly successful. One thing that was abrasively clear to me though was that, besides those who had done this before, the newbies needed extensive training before we reached out to the pub-

1

lic. Weekly PEACE meetings began where I created power points about different animal agriculture industries and presented them to the group, then we discussed.

Within this time period, I became restless. One day I saw a transport truck full of pigs driving through town and I decided to follow them. They led me straight into the depths of CAFO territory, which was a new term to me at this time. It stands for Concentrated Animal Feeding Operation, also known as a factory farm. It's the term the industries like to use because most people simply don't know what it stands for. Where I was on the road, there were miles of massive metal buildings holding tens of thousands of animals within those walls. That was the first day I saw the inside of one of these farms in real life.

It was summer, and the massive curtains that covered the fenced in windows were open, allowing the cries of the pigs, the stench of their feces and the sight of their suffering to be seen. I looked into the eyes of these animals and felt a part of me shatter. We did this to them. Unless someone rescued them from this facility, then this is where they would spend their entire life up until slaughter. That was, if they were so unlucky to live that long. To my right was a sight I had never witnessed before: a dumpster full of rotting corpses. The conditions in these farms are absolutely horrific, so much so that many of the animals living in this confinement never make it out alive.

I took pictures of those I could, printed them out, and showed up to a hearing in the courthouse twenty minutes later regarding the construction of a new mega CAFO near the town's main water source. Dozens of people flooded the courtroom, practically all of them opposing the facility. They cited numerous environmental issues and an increase in the disgusting stench that would often waft into town. All of these reasons were valid but they just weren't why I was there. When I stood up I brought up the perspective of the animals. I reminded people that the real victims of these facilities are those being forced to live, and often die, inside of them. All of the environmental effects are byproducts of an operation designed to be oppressive.

The CAFO ended up being built. Worse yet, the council we begged to deny the permit, fast tracked the operation. What's deeply unfortunate, is that in a state like Iowa, where we have well over ten thousand registered CAFOs, big ag essentially owns the government. Massive financial contributions are made to politicians by CAFO f(h)armers, which incentivizes them to approve whatever project they propose - no matter how much the public begs them not to.

The night after the court hearing my mind was racing. In one of the facilities I saw that day, there were well over a thousand individuals. I wanted to save them all. Unfortunately, that seemed quite impossible: A) because it is highly illegal and if I get caught I would most likely be charged with the animal enterprise terrorism act and jailed indefinitely, b) because I don't have a car big enough to fit more than one full grown pig, and c) because I would have nowhere to take the rescued animals.

I, however, am not one to take no for an answer.

That night, after a student government meeting the idea emerged. What if we purchased the entire CAFO, with the pigs inside, turned it into a sanctuary and built an ecovillage from the ground up on the surrounding land. We could liberate all of those inside destined to become someone's 60 seconds of pleasure, regenerate the land and provide a peaceful home where we can all live in harmony with the earth, animals and ourselves. This place would be called Home.

"Home" became my final project in the global solutions class I was participating in and I dedicated everything to it. One major factor was money. I would need millions of dollars to start and complete this project, along with a community of people all motivated to do the same. In one of our peace meetings we began discussing how we could possibly do this. Someone mentioned that we didn't have a vegan restaurant in town, and that that may be a good way to raise money, spread the vegan message and build community.

Within a month, I signed the lease that evolved into Plant. Ambitious? Yes. But I heard that a burger place was looking to rent it and I wasn't going to let them take a location that appeared perfect to me at the time. The following months were filled with writing a business plan, figuring out recipes, solidifying the legalities and all of the other tiny details that go into a restaurant. I, myself, had never even worked in a proper restaurant before. So it was all quite new to me.

After a year at MIU, I dropped out to work at Plant full time. We began throwing raves to raise money before fully opening, which were absolutely iconic if I do say so myself. Within a month of officially opening, we hosted Marianne Williamson to speak in our theater, who was running for president at the time.

The beginning of Plant was filled with hard work, hours of planning and not a lot of time at home. The idea of a restaurant had evolved into a community event center, theater, kava lounge, art gallery & of course, vegan restaurant. When we first opened, I had us open every day from 11am to 9pm most days. This schedule quickly proved fatal and so we closed Thursdays.

The many people that I hired quickly turned into a volunteer system due to my gross overestimation of how much cash flow would be coming in. And when the first wave of COVID-19 entered Iowa and we were ordered to do take-out only, I declared we would close for two weeks. In all honesty, COVID saved my sanity at the time. I remember reading the notification while in the bathroom, running out and yelling to my coworker and friend, Jio, " lock the doors. We're closed!" We then sat in the cuddle corner and watched Netflix for hours.

Covid-19 hit about three months after we fully opened, which significantly impacted our plans moving forward. For a while we offered carry out only, then eventually allowed people to dine in once again. The schedule in our final months of operation were Friday - Sunday, since those were our busiest days. This also allowed me time to simply exist and also pursue my other passion, which is reiki. My partner, Justin, and I are both energy healers, so on weekdays we held energy healing sessions and weekends were spent at Plant. This schedule was much more livable compared to how I started in the beginning, however, Plant just isn't what I'd first imagined it would be.

Many people warned me to not open a restaurant. They said that it has the lowest profit margins and that it takes years to even make any money at all. I believed that Plant would be the exception and that we would thrive. Now that I've been paying the rent out of pocket for well over a year and working tirelessly to lose a lot of money I see what they were saying.

I absolutely love Plant. I love the people who come in and the meals we serve and the community that supports us. I love the art on our walls and all the parties we've thrown, events we've hosted and the living vision that we are. A conversation with my mom, however, highlighted the ways in which I was giving too much of myself for this business.

The second part of my vision has always been to travel to various eco villages, sanctuaries and organic farms around the world to learn from them. I want to know what works and what doesn't. I want to get my hands dirty and learn how to plant something that can feed my community. I want to learn basic animal care and the how-tos of owning a sanctuary. I want to gather this knowledge so that when the time comes to build with my community, I'll know what I'm doing. I want to experience the world while I still can. So I'm going to.

In this life, we never really know how much time we have. Every moment is a gift. And I realized that while I love Plant dearly, it was no longer life affirming for me. Spending hours upon hours inside a brick building, devoid of sunlight, was exhausting and consumed a majority of my mental space. I felt trapped. So I chose me, which is why I'm writing this book. As I write these words, it is March 17th of 2021. Plant closes almost exactly a month from now.

Writing that feels weird, but it's the reality of the situation. I didn't want to simply leave the people I love empty handed, so I offer you this book. It contains all of our recipes, as well as vegan resources and information on activism & animal agriculture.

The next section of this book will be that. If you're wondering why I am vegan, or why this mission is important to me and many others, then I ask you to read on.

My Journey To Veganism

What is veganism? Many people have different answers to this question. The definition we will be using, as stated by the Vegan Society, is as follows:

""Veganism is a philosophy and way of living which seeks to exclude—as far as is possible and practicable—all forms of exploitation of, and cruelty to, animals for food, clothing or any other purpose; and by extension, promotes the development and use of animal-free alternatives for the benefit of animals, humans and the environment. In dietary terms it denotes the practice of dispensing with all products derived wholly or partly from animals."

I, like many of my fellow humans, was raised on a diet that consisted heavily of animal products. I was the self-proclaimed "biggest meat eater" in my family, actually. I ate steak at least once a week and loved bacon, chicken, ribs and the whole allotment of dairy products. Simultaneously, since I first watched the show Animal Cops, I wanted to rescue animals. I had dreams of being an Animal Cop or a veterinarian or a marine biologist or of owning a sanctuary. I adored every animal I met, despised hunting and felt that I advocated for the proper treatment of animals.

Ironic, huh?

It quite frankly never crossed my mind that my diet was having a direct impact on the lives of animals in an abrasively harmful manner. My common excuse was, " well they're already dead, so it would be disrespectful not to eat them." I, of course, would never apply that same logic to our beloved pets at home, but felt it justified my meat intake. At this time I was wholly unaware of the impact of the industries I supported each and every day.

Throughout my life, I've also been overweight. My body type is modeled after my father: tall, broad shoulders, muscular & easily able to store fat. Since middle school, I'd go on multiple diets cutting calories and carbs and sugars, but never meat. Nothing ever seemed to stick. By the age of 13 a doctor informed me that I was pre-diabetic, had high "bad cholesterol" levels and that the experiences I was having (where I would wake up feeling nauseous, light headed and shaking) were due to hypoglycemia. Health wise, I was a wreck, and emotionally, I was in the same boat.

One day, when I was 16, I felt terribly ill. For the next couple weeks, the only thing my body was able to accept happily was smoothies and on occasion saltines. It was a much needed cleanse and afterwards I felt significantly better. Something strange happened in that time period though, my craving for meat had disappeared. I just didn't want it anymore. I started loosely classifying myself as vegetarian, which I felt made sense due to my love for animals. I would occasionally have pepperoni on pizza when my boyfriend at the time ordered it, but for the most part I was meat free.

I recall the last time I ate meat distinctly. It was after taking my brother to a youth group. My blood sugar fell during the meeting, where

I also grew very agitated at the pastor for basically telling a group of children that all sexual desires and acts were sinful before marriage. I was pissed and needed to eat something to ground me. There was an Applebee's near us, so we drove over and ordered. I got the steak and mashed potatoes because I felt my body needed something "nutritious". I probably took no more than three bites of it before swearing off meat for the rest of my life. I was disgusted. This hunk of flesh that once appealed to me greatly was now revolting. Turns out the potatoes and side of vegetables were all my body needed to stabilize anyways.

Several months passed of being casually vegetarian when Summer rolled around. Every year, my family on my dad's side would go on a little vacation together for about a week. This year, we stayed at a lake house in Idaho. It was during this trip, when I was scrolling through Instagram and Liam Hemsworth posted a picture of the documentary "What the Health". I'd been seeing it pop up on my recommended movies, so I was immediately interested. His caption said something like: "If you care about the planet, your health or animals then watch this. If you don't, then still watch it."

As someone who cared deeply about all of the above, I decided to give it a-go. I basically live-streamed the entire movie on my Snapchat with my commentary because of how appalled I was. Everything I had ever learned about health and nutrition was a lie. It was no wonder my health had gone to such shit! Halfway through the film I made the decision to go vegan. After it ended I rushed upstairs to my mother, having just finished crying, and declared that I was now Vegan. She sort of shrugged it off, as she assumed it was just another diet fad I would do for a week. Flustered, I returned to my room and watched the documentary again, taking 19 pages of notes. Then, I followed about 100 vegans on twitter.

Within a month, my health shifted dramatically. I was no longer having hypoglycemic episodes, and I started naturally losing weight. I did quickly find vegan junk food, so the weight loss wasn't too significant. What was significant, however, was what happened internally. When I got my blood drawn it showed that I was no longer pre diabetic and my cholesterol levels had left the danger zone. This makes sense when you factor in that cholesterol is only found in animal products. Upon seeing the effect this lifestyle was having on me and my newfound passion for veganism, my mom decided to make the switch as well.

Around that same time, I began to feel uncomfortable with my passive lifestyle. I loved the diet I had adopted; however, I felt there was more I could be doing. Some of the people I had followed online shared footage from something they called a Vigil, where they stood outside of slaughterhouses and tried to give animals water and love before they were sent to slaughter. Something awakened inside of me upon seeing this and I suddenly realized how much I wasn't doing. Yes, I was no longer paying for these animals to be killed.. but I wasn't doing anything to stop it.

I quickly found a local activist group, Portland Animal Save, and contacted them. One of the organizers and now dear friend, Emily, informed me that they were having a vigil that Wednesday. I was distraught because I had class at that time period, and I couldn't ditch because I was responsible for driving two of my friends to class as well. We were all in something called Running Start, a program where you take college classes your last two year of Highschool, so we drove about a 25 minute commute together.

I promised myself I would go to the one occurring the following weekend, and that night engaged in a documentary called Earthlings. It shattered me. This film (which you can watch for free online at nation-earth.com) clearly showed the reality and depth of the animal industries - ranging from animals raised for food, clothing, entertainment, companionship, racing & cosmetic testing. A majority of the information shown to me was completely new to my world, and it made me realize just how important taking action is. It is literally a life or death decision.

The next day I drove my friends to class and sat in the hard seat, listening to our teacher talk about human evolution and feeling a panic attack build. My attention wouldn't leave the clock. I watched the time get closer and closer to the start of the vigil and I felt my guilt creep in for not being present. There were animals at that very moment being sent to slaughter. Their life would come to a brutal end that day, and I had the opportunity to at least show them a hint of compassion before they were murdered.

When class ended I left. I told my friends I would pick them up at the end of the day and I skipped my following classes, driving quickly to the vigil. I cried a lot during the hour drive there. When I arrived, I was met with a small group of activists holding signs on the side of an off-ramp. I was informed that this is where most of the trucks headed to the nearby slaughterhouse come off the freeway and were often stopped at a red light. This gave us a brief opportunity to film the animals inside of the trailer and give them a chance to be seen as more than a slab of meat. It wasn't easy. Looking at someone, knowing their life is about to be taken from them and you can't do anything other than bear witness is horrible. But I believe that in order to change this system, it is necessary. We must bear witness to the atrocities our species is committing before being able to revolutionize and liberate the oppressive system. We must recognize there is a problem and truly understand it's depth in order to create and facilitate a solution.

That is the day I became an activist and truly understood what veganism meant. Before that day, I had one place I would "cheat at". It was Olive Garden. I am a lover of fettuccini Alfredo and even though theirs was riddled with animal products, I felt that my occasional cheat wasn't doing any real harm. At this point, I still didn't really understand the dairy industry. However, after seeing truck after truck of "spent" dairy cows with painfully massive udders being sent to the slaughterhouse after their existence is deemed unprofitable, my actions finally aligned with my ethics.

Veganism is about much more than simply eating plants, being healthy and helping the environment. It is often all of those things, but it's scope is much greater. Veganism is a liberatory lifestyle. One that aims to transform the violent system we operate within into one of peace. It focuses on abolishing all forms of slavery, that which is done unto non-human animals, humans and the environment. The scope of harm that these animal exploitation industries have caused is enormous. Ranging from the obvious violence unto animals, to the exploitation of workers, degradation of our earth, pollution of our waters, and deadly effects on our bodies. That is what we will be addressing next. But before we do, I would like to preface with an ounce of hope.

We are all creators who have the potential and capability to make a great impact on those we connect with and the planet we call home. We have the power to change lives, influence minds, love fiercely and devote ourselves to causes we feel called to. For many of us, when we look at the state of the world we see chaos. Sometimes I am overwhelmed by the immense amount of suffering I see. It happened quite a few times while writing this book. There will be many scientific estimates I will be mentioning in the following chapters that feel quite doomsday-y. And truly, they can be. That, however, is only if we continue on this path.

I believe that we are powerful beings. We have the power to love and to hate, to destroy and to create, to care for and to exploit, to help and to harm. We have the power of choice, and our choices are interconnected with those we share this conscious experience with. Our choices have a seemingly never-ending domino effect that can and do completely alter the timeline we are in alignment with.

Quantum physics teaches us that infinite possibilities exist in every situation. Some of which are predictable, while others transcend our wildest dreams. A future in which we plant billions of trees and tend to the earth, care for our fellow earthlings and live in harmony with one another is within the realm of these possibilities. As is the timeline in which we nuke ourselves into oblivion, either with literal nuclear weapons or by continuing our harmful behaviors and passive patterns that essentially require our planet to abort us. The latter is receiving a mass amount of attention currently, but I worry that this is a dangerous form of mass manifestation. I, for one, am actively choosing to live in the former reality. I believe in us.

One person has an insurmountably large impact. We affect each and every being we come into contact with. The scope and scale of that effect depends greatly on the depth of that interaction. Think about that one person you know who just seems like a beaming ray of sunshine. When you're around them you almost can't help but to be happy. Their energy is contagious, infectious even. Imagine if we all radiated that kind of light. Imagine if hope spread faster than any virus ever could.

What would that look like?

A world where we support one another, and achieve our goals. A world where we care for our neighbors, including our nonhuman ones. A world where more people hug trees and kiss the ground with their bare feet. A world where healthcare is holistic and our diets are filled with the colors of the rainbow that grow freely on our beautiful earth. A world where we are warm to those we have not yet met, and welcome them into our hearts excitedly. A world of true peace and boundless prosperity. This world is possible.

Would you like to see it come to life?

I would love to build this world with you. In order to do so, I feel that we are in need of a comprehensive understanding of the state of the world now and the areas that are in desperate need of loving transformation. This next section of the book will be overlooking the affects our actions have on the lives of trillions of animals around the globe, some of which may be in your backyard. I do not intend to frighten you with this information, but to inform you so that as we move forward we can do so with a clear goal and mutual understanding of why certain changes are necessary in order to actualize this vision of world peace.

I ask you to be present and to reflect on what I'm about to share with you. Do further research into what you feel called to and ask questions. Write them down. Ponder the knowledge shared and inquire within yourself if you are a willing or unwilling participant of some of the topics discussed and what you can do about it. Please keep an open mind and hopeful heart as we dive in. We will be creating solutions once we truly understand the problem at hand.

Thank you for your presence.

The Reality of Animal Agriculture

"Our treatment of animals is not simply cruel and inhumane: it reflects a deeply destructive culture in which animals are bred — and genetically engineered — into units of economic and social convenience. In the process, we destroy our own animal spirit, producing a creature-less mechanical society. To create meaningful change we must see animals and nature as our equals, rather than ingredients for industrial progress."[1]

Let's talk numbers. According to the United Nations, approximately 70 billion land animals and 2.7 *trillion* sea creatures are killed for food every year. Mind you, this number doesn't include any other animals killed for cosmetic and medical testing, clothing, entertainment, land management, etc. In the US, 99% of all animals used for food are raised in factory farms, while globally this number is 90%.[2] The following information is based on industry standards of how humans use and abuse other species. These are not rare instances. This is unfortunately standard practice, and while you may or may not be the one literally slitting the throat of an animal, stealing their children or confining them in tight spaces, to quote Andrew Kimbrell, " Factory farms, like environmental pollution, are representative of numerous systematic industrial evils that only 1 percent of society creates but in which the other 99 percent are complicit."[3]

I'd like to begin by cultivating a deeper understanding of why modern day farming is as it is. The birth of confinement-based agriculture came from the end of World War II for both the United States & Europe. At this point in history, many people abandoned farming practices due to economic and environmental hardship. A fear began encroaching on the collective consciousness of a depleting food supply. This fear was lulled by new technologies that were emerging, which allowed farming practices to evolve (or perhaps, devolve).

Animals were moved in-doors, so that their environment could be controlled and less land would be required to attain an attractive profit margin. Humans were replaced with machines whenever possible and the amount of animals on a single farm steadily multiplied. The modern day factory farm was born. Prior to this shift, a farmer could make a living on the backs of 50 dairy cows.[4] Now, more than a thousand are generally required to be profitable. This makes it so that even those who want to take a more naturalistic approach to agriculture cannot do so without losing money. These people also generally have no interest in working in Concentrated Animal Feeding Operations due to their poor standard of living for the animals and working environment for the employees. This results in people who are generally unknowledgeable in animal care working on these facilities and learning as they go. Since profit is now the #1 priority, they hire the cheapest workers they can find, which on average are undocumented immigrants.

In these new confinement-based farms where the natural behaviors of animals were greatly suppressed and diseases ran rampant, the solutions that were implemented were essentially just as harmful as the problem. A slew of vaccines, hormones and antibiotics are injected into all of these animals just to keep them alive long enough to be slaughtered. Neurotic conditions developed in many animals due to the insanity of their living conditions. Chickens would peck one another to death, so the solution was to cut off the ends of their beaks on their first day of life with zero pain killers. Pigs would bite one another's tails, so farmers responded by cutting them off as infants.

In order to be considered a CAFO, there must be 1,000 or more "animal units" within the facility. Anything smaller is considered an Animal Feeding Operation (AFO). The scale of some of these factory farms is almost unimaginable. " Cal- Maine, the largest egg producer in the United States, sold 685 million dozen eggs in 2007 and keeps a flock of 23 million layers."[5] Some egg-laying facilities imprison up to 130,000 hens. Individual care is nonexistent, and those displaying weakness, abnormalities or illness are culled (killed). Cows used in the dairy industry within the U.S. are culled at a rate of 20% every year.[5]

Alongside the egregious animal abuse occurring within these facilities, the environment around them suffers immensely as well. This is a topic I will be diving deeper into during the environmental section of this book; however, I feel it's important to discuss why they're able to get away with grossly mismanaged waste and polluting the environment.

The CAFO lobbyists have done an excellent job at ensuring local and state laws are in the favor of their employers. Since CAFOs are legally viewed as an agricultural enterprise, they are largely immune from environmental protection laws in the U.S, such as the Clean Air Act and the Clean Water Act.[5] If they were to be considered an industrial enterprise, then they would be forced to regulate their pollution levels and pay for the cleanup costs that their destructive operation ensues. This is why the industry prefers the term Concentrated Animal Feeding Operation opposed to Factory Farm. Because if they were truly viewed as and treated as a factory then they would not be able to get away with as much as they presently do.

While most people, including those who work in traditional farming practices, agree that the present system of industrialized animal agriculture is brutal and heartless, I'd like to challenge the notion that the solution is to return to our previous ways of "animal husbandry". I'll begin with a quote from the book CAFO regarding the relationship between farmers and animals, " … The result is good animal husbandry: a fair and mutually beneficial contract between humans and animals, each better off because of the relationship."[4]

Now, let's break this down a bit. In order for a contract to be formed there must be some form of consent from both parties involved. When members of either party don't speak the same language, it's a bit difficult to truly know what was agreed to and what was not. The last sentence quoted really struck a chord with me… because the animals end up dead. Not just dead, but murdered by the very person who has protected them. Their supposed guardian then becomes their killer or the person who sends them to a brutal death. I cannot see how that is either fair or mutually beneficial. I do not believe that caring for someone with the intention to kill them for the use of their flesh is somehow respectable. While there is, of course, a drastic difference in the manner in which animals are raised, the end result is still there. If we were to apply this same notion to humans, it would be unacceptable. I would like to challenge us to extend that same manner of thinking unto our fellow earthlings.

Speciesism

Before we dive into the deep end, I'd like to address a lesser known form of discrimination: speciesism. In essence, speciesism is the assumption of human superiority that leads to the oppression of nonhuman animals. This also applies to the way we view certain species versus others based on the culture we were raised in. As a species, we have other-ized animals, despite the fact that we ourselves are animals. Most of us view animals as less than, different, subjectable, obedient, unintelligent and worst of all: property. So, when a human is called an "animal" or a "bitch" or a "cow," the ingrained, automatic response is to take offense. That is due to how deeply speciesism is embedded into our language.

Speciesism, similar to all other isms, is a system of oppression that privileges and over-values human beings while it disadvantages and under-values non-human animals. Speciesism is an agent-target system in which every single human being on this planet is an agent, regardless of sex, gender, class, race, ability or any other distinction. As the agent in an unjust system, it is our responsibility to check our privilege and see what we can do for those who have lost rights due to our privilege. Quite frankly, the least we can do is stop paying for their enslavement.

Speciesism is quite applicable to the privileges humans attain over nonhuman animals, but it is also seen in our emotional relationship to animals. Most people care more deeply for dogs than they do fish, for cats than they do cows, for horses than they do pigs. Person to person this differs, as we all have different emotional experiences and therefore varying associations with our animal kin. What is important to note is that the inherent value of someone's life and wellbeing is not determined by our relationship to them.

There are quite literally billions of humans on this planet that you will never meet in this lifetime; however, that doesn't take away from the value of their life. You may not be sad if they were to pass on as you did not know them, but their life still matters. The same thought system can be applied to all animals. All of our lives are special to us. Our experiences are our own and we have the right to be happy, to enjoy life. Who are we to take away another's life, another's joy?

Fish

On commercial farms, anywhere between 37 and 120 billion fish are killed annually.[1] While in the wild, well over two trillion fish face a brutal death. Fish are killed and consumed more than any other animal on the planet. They are also the most popular pet and they are the second most common vertebrae used for animal testing. There are approximately 32,000 known species of fish and records show that they've been here on earth for around 500 million years.[2]

In our ignorance, humans often classify all fish as being unintelligent and incapable of suffering. This is a gross misperception, as some fish have been observed following traditions, holding long term memories, working with one another and even using tools.[3] The range at which sea creatures differ is similar to how us land mammals do the same. Humans are different from kangaroos as goldfish are different from the largetooth sawfish. We're all individuals within our common species having a unique experience in this world.

As land animals, we often don't connect to our fellow earthlings in the sea. Many people at least passively care about the lives of whales and dolphins; however, when it comes to fish, most of us are apathetic due to our lack of emotional connection to these creatures. How might our behavior change if we had an idea of what their lives were like?

I'd like to ask you this: do you believe that your emotional connection to someone determines the inherent value of their life? Does a lack of connection to someone justify their life being stolen from them?

Imagine for a moment what it would be like to be ripped from your home by a hook in the mouth and brought into a new world in which you cannot breathe and the first creature you encounter shows you merciless brutality. Can you feel the panic in that encounter? The fear?

Is that what fish feel?

Perhaps you're thinking, "do fish even feel pain?" The short answer to that is, yes. There has been quite a bit of research conducted on the matter and the general consensus of the scientific community is that fish do in fact have the ability to suffer. If you would like to look more into the matter then I suggest reading an article in the Smithsonian magazine online titled "It's Official: Fish Feel Pain."[4]

Despite the overwhelming evidence that fish suffer when us humans do horrific things to them, they still have practically no legal protection, especially on factory farms. These intensive farming operations, also known as aquaculture, make up about half of all sea life consumed by humans. Antibiotics, hormones and pesticides are used habitually on the fish to keep diseases at bay in the overcrowded, dirty environment they are kept in.[5]

In open ocean aquacultures', all of the chemicals that aren't absorbed into the fish being farmed seeps out into the sea. This is obviously harmful for the environment. Additionally, on occasion one of the caged fish may make a successful escape. While that is excellent for that individual, it may have a detrimental effect on the native life, as diseases or unideal genetic traits may be spread to wild fish.

Most fish farmed industrially are carnivorous. Several pounds of wild fish are sometimes consumed to produce one pound of farmed fish. Fish such as Bluefin Tuna's are considered highly efficient ocean predators, but now because one can be sold for *millions of dollars,* they are being killed at unprecedented rates. Another example of this is the living dinosaur of the sea, Sturgeon.

These great beasts can grow up to 6 meters in length in the wild and live to be 100 years old. Biologists have uncovered evidence suggesting that Sturgeon were alive over 200 million years ago.[6] Despite this, the inflated superiority complex of humankind still farms and kills these creatures. Why? Well, mostly for their eggs.

Often farmed indoors for a period of 1-7 years, Sturgeon are exploited for their sexual reproductive systems and their flesh. After being yanked out of the not so safe environment they were forcibly bred into and whacked in the head with a hammer, they are dismembered. Their eggs are taken out of them to be sold as caviar, their bladder is removed and often used to filter beer, and their flesh is sold as meat.

Humans annihilate species at all levels of the ecological hierarchy. While slaughtering top predators is awful, killing the animals serving as the baseline food source for many sea creatures is equally, if not more, destructive. Due to this, the Antarctic ecosystem is critically endangered, largely because of climate change & a key species being at risk: krill. Krill are essential for the survival of several large marine species, such as whales & penguins.[7]

Global warming has been making the sea less friendly for these little critters, while fishing has taken a deadly toll on their numbers. The main purpose for these invertebrates industrially is as fish feed and for health supplements. Some massive fishing ships, which act as floating slaughterhouses, essentially vacuum millions of krill from the ocean. Those who capture and kill krill estimate that there are 400-500 million tons of krill left. However, an estimate from the British Antarctic Survey has a much lower estimate of 110 million tons. This is deeply concerning when the legal catch limit is put at 4 million tons. A marine reserves expert with GreenPeace International states that, " Whales, penguins, seals, albatrosses and petrels — all those creatures we think are absolute icons of Antarctica — depend on krill. It's part of the global commons, and one of the most pristine environments on Earth."[8]

In addition to the obvious violence committed against fish in the fishing industry, there are ways in which this slaughter has a ripple effect across the entire world. Let's start with our coral reefs. Coral reefs are a collection of living animals that thrive off of fish excrement, while also serving as the home for many fish. They have a symbiotic relationship that is dependent upon one another. Unfortunately, due to an array of factors including fishing, rising sea temperatures, ocean dead zones and general pollutants, the world's coral reefs are dying off at unprecedented rates. In the great barrier reef, at least a quarter of the coral is dying. Globally, half of the oceans coral reefs have died off and the trajectory moving forward appears to be grim.[9] With the coral reefs of the ocean dying, it points to disaster for our planet's seas and for all those who rely on them.

In addition to coral loss, the death of the ocean may very well mean the death of the planet as we know it. Estimates by scientists state that

50-80% of the oxygen on Earth is produced by ocean life. The oxygen produced fluctuates and much of it is consumed by ocean life themselves; however, when dead zones emerge (areas in which more oxygen is consumed than is produced) then a dangerous situation arises. Sea creatures are unable to live in a dead zone, so that area becomes devoid of life.[10]

As of 2008 405 dead zones were recorded in a study; many of which surrounded the coasts of the United States. Dead Zones can happen naturally, but most do not. Dead Zones are caused by an increased amount of chemical nutrients in the ocean which leads to an excessive algae bloom. Once these algae die, the matter begins to decompose. This process takes up quite a bit of oxygen, and when there's an abundance of algae then it can sometimes take a majority of the oxygen contained in the surrounding ocean. This leads to water with a severe lack of oxygen, which makes it an unlivable habitat for sea life.[11]

Animal waste, which is rich with nutrients and chemicals, that is improperly disposed of makes its way into our oceans. Often massive factory farms are next to rivers, streams and major water sources that eventually lead into the ocean. This is why there are massive dead zones surrounding the entire southern and eastern coastlines of the United States. In this country alone, the US Environmental Protection Agency estimates that 335 million tons of manure is created by livestock annually. In North Carolina alone, the manure produced by pigs is more than double that of the human population there - and that is all managed without a proper waste treatment plant! This shitload of manure paired with fertilizer run off from the mass amounts of chemically treated monocrops creates a toxic mixture for our oceans. This is seen as the leading cause of ocean dead zones.[11]

Now, let's address carbon for a moment. Carbon is a trace gas that traps heat within the atmosphere. Put simply, too much carbon in the atmosphere leads to rising temperatures across the globe. This could cause a chain reaction that would dramatically change life on this planet as we know it.

The ocean is capable of absorbing 50% of the carbon being emitted, being the largest carbon sink on the planet. This makes sense, as the ocean covers 70% of our planet. The ocean hasn't always had to be a carbon sink; however, human activity has led to this major role being adopted. The ocean does naturally absorb carbon, however it does have it's limit and when that is reached, ocean acidification is the result . With that said, the ocean is absolutely vital in order to keep global temperatures livable for a majority of the species that call this planet home.[12]

Plankton, coral, fish and algae absorb carbon from the atmosphere. Larger fish, such as whales, absorb mass amounts of carbon from the atmosphere. This means that sea life staying in the ocean is essential in order for carbon sequestration to occur. Less sea life equals more carbon in the atmosphere. Now, keep that in mind for this next sentence.

If current fishing trends continue, it is likely that the ocean will be devoid of practically all reachable life by 2048.[13]

When we fish, we are not only taking a life but we are also taking carbon out of the ocean and putting it back into our atmosphere. When it comes to whaling, this matter becomes much more severe. Sea creatures serve a vital role for the balance of our planet. Approximately 93% of carbon stored can be found in the oceans. We need it to stay there.

Bycatch

"Nearly 300 wild sea animals are killed every year to feed one American, but that doesn't include the fishing industry's bycatch."[1]

Bycatch is the number of sea creatures that fishermen didn't intend to catch, but did so anyway. They are often caught in the large nets of industrial fishers, used to sweep the bottom of the ocean floor. Those unintentionally caught are then discarded, often dead or injured, back into the ocean. These animals can include dolphins, turtles, sharks, sting rays, anchovies and krill - to name a few. When you factor in the number of animals caught inadvertently to the kill count of the average American's diet, then the number of deaths jumps to 500 sea animals a year... for just one human.[1]

Shrimp trawler nets, specifically, are devastating for the environment. Nearly two thirds of the beings caught in these death traps are considered bycatch and are often discarded back into the ocean dead. Those who were caught intentionally generally die of asphyxiation (choking due to lack of oxygen), while the rest are gutted alive. Time of death after being caught ranges from 25 to 250 minutes.

Of those killed, nearly half of them are used as "feed fish," that is, fish used to feed other animals that will then be fed to humans. These animals include other fish, chickens and pigs.

Whales

Whales are incredible creatures. They are emotionally complex and have specific neurons that are linked to communication, memory, perception, understanding and problem solving. Evolutionary scientists theorize that they used to be land animals that returned to the sea over a long period of time.

Blue Whales are the largest known animal on the planet. Their tongue weighs about as much as their nearest competitor - the elephant. These whales sing throughout the day in a language that humans only dream to understand. It's been theorized that if there was no land mass to block it, then a blue whales song could circle the entire globe and return to the original singer. Toothed whales (including dolphins) use echolocation to identify where others are in their environment and to navigate the underwater terrain.[1]

Whales experience a level of protection that most species do not. In 1986 commercial whaling was banned; however, three countries still continue whaling. These nations are Japan, Norway and Iceland. Since the ban, they've killed around 40,000 whales for the purposes of scientific investigation and food.[2]

An activist group dedicated to marine life, the Sea Shepherds, has been leading the fight against whaling. They have been particularly active in harassing Japanese commercial whaling ships posing as research vessels. The place they chose to hunt was in the Southern Ocean Whale Sanctuary. Between the years 2002-2017, the Sea Shepherds have directly stopped the attempted murder of 6,000 whales. For this reason, the Sea Shepherds are unjustly labeled as eco-terrorists.[3]

Another aspect of this industry is the whales and dolphins taken for entertainment. As of March 15th, 2021, at least 59 orcas are held in captivity. 27 of them were captured in the wild, taken from their families, and destined to live in a fish tank for the rest of their life. 32 of these animals were born into these caged conditions. Since 1961, 166 orcas have been taken from captivity. 129 of them are now dead. This becomes increasingly upsetting when the natural lifespan of these beings is considered.

Males: average of 30 years, can live to be 60
Females: average of 46 years, can live to be 90

Presently, Seaworld has twenty orcas in their three parks and at least 49 orcas have died in their care. One orca, who was caught at the young age of four is still being kept as their slave. In 1977, she was captured along with over 80 other residents of the southern sea. Seven were taken into captivity while at least five died. Known now by her captors as Lolita, she is the only survivor.[4] The Southern Resident Orcas are now a critically endangered population. Recently many of them have slowly starved to death due to overfishing. Pods are often seen sharing fish when they are having trouble finding food. One of their oldest members was seen doing this before dying of starvation. If we don't stop taking animals from the ocean, then in the near future there will no longer be life in the ocean. If that happens, then it is our fault for not taking action, which we absolutely still can.

After the documentary's release he stated that his words were taken out of context. According to Intrafish he said, " "I answered that there are no guarantees in life, but that by drastically reducing the number of vessels intentionally chasing and netting dolphins as well as other regulations in place, that the number of dolphins that are killed is very low."[6]

Now, while it's nice that fewer boats are intentionally hunting and killing dolphins, that does not actually take away from his previous statement. While this organization has worked to successfully decline the number of dolphins killed in the tuna industry, there is no guarantee that your "dolphin-safe tuna" label is in fact what it claims to be. And regardless of if a dolphin did or did not die, that Tuna probably would have preferred to live as well.

In addition to the harm done to dolphins via fishing, many are kidnapped from the wild and taken to live as captives in aquariums for the purpose of entertainment. In these aquariums, they are generally trained to perform. Often, they are taught how to do tricks through methods of food deprivation. In essence, they keep the dolphins hungry so that they'll do just about anything for their next meal. They are kept in small tanks in unfamiliar pod groupings, completely isolated from their natural habitat and lifestyle. Many die young due to the extremely stressful environment. Virtually all of them are deeply traumatized from the events that unfolded, leading to their capture.

In Taiji, Japan there is an annual dolphin slaughter and capture that lasts six months. This massacre takes place in a cove near an ancient migratory route of theirs. What's important to note before I describe their method of capture is this: sound is the primary sense of dolphins. Their sonar is so powerful that they can literally see through solid masses with their incredible perception. This power is used against them.

The fishermen wait along dolphin migratory paths and bang massive poles on the boats and form a wall of sound forcing the dolphins into the cove. They then leave a net up and go. The dolphins spend the night captured and distressed. The next morning dolphin trainers select the ones they want. They collect young females primarily, then fly them to different parts of the world. This is a multi million dollar industry.

Instead of releasing the rest of the unchosen, they murder them all. This process takes about half an hour. They are all stabbed again and again and again until they die. The blue water turns a dark crimson red as each of the dolphins slowly bleeds out into the water. It is agonizingly slow, violent and unnecessarily cruel. This reality is highlighted by the fact that dolphin meat is not commonly eaten in Japan. Most Japanese citizens are wholly unaware of this slaughter and when this information is brought to their attention they are disgusted. Meanwhile, those who do eat dolphin flesh are being slowly poisoned by the high levels of mercury contained in their flesh.

A group of activists in Japan made a documentary about this titled The Cove[2]. Ric O'Barry was one of the most prominent figures in the film, particularly because of his background. Ric both captured and trained 5 dolphins used in the popular TV series Flipper. He developed a deep connection with these dolphins over a period of many years due to his role. One day, the dolphin he lived beside swam into his arms and stopped breathing. Every breath a dolphin takes is a conscious effort. This means that at this moment, after years of captivity, she chose to die in his arms.

That night he was arrested attempting to free captive dolphins. It is now his mission to free every captive dolphin he can and to end the slaughter in Taiji. The reason Taiji is his focus is due to the fact that it is where the most dolphins are captured and killed in the world. You may be wondering why the fishers choose to kill them when their flesh is not commonly consumed and therefore not worth much. The answer is truly saddening.

They are seen as pests.

Dolphins eat fish, and with a global fish population rapidly declining due to human activity there is fear among the fishermen that soon the sea will run dry. That fear is then displaced onto the creatures that actually need fish to survive. One year, activists offered to give the fishermen the same amount of money they would get for killing dolphins, to *not go*. They said it wasn't about the amount of money, it was about "pest control". The government paid them to kill massive amounts of dolphins because they "eat too much fish".[2]

Sharks

Well over 500 species of sharks live in the ocean and have been doing so since the age of the dinosaurs.[1] Every shark species is a completely different creature, with Lantern sharks being about the size of a human hand and Whale Sharks looking more like a bus. Hammerheads' unique, elongated heads give them nearly 360 degree vision and the ability to sense electromagnetic fields.[2] Some sharks lay eggs while others give live births. The duration of their pregnancies range from months for some to several years for others. Their lifespans vary greatly as well, with the most impressive being the GreenLand Shark. Scientists estimate they can live to be 500 years old. The differing skills, capabilities and purposes these creatures serve in their given ecosystems are truly amazing. In most spaces they occupy, sharks are apex predators and are absolutely essential to maintain the delicate balance of the ocean's health.

Unfortunately, at least 100 million sharks are killed every year. That number only factors in those reported, as it is estimated that millions more are killed illegally. This continuous massacre has led to a third of all shark species (around 181 of them) being labeled as endangered.[3] Sharks are often directly killed for their fins, meat, liver oil and cartilage while also being indirectly killed as bycatch.[4]

Shark fin soup is seen as a status symbol in parts of Asia and is used in Traditional Chinese Medicine. A bowl of shark fin soup can go for up to

$100, despite the cartilage itself being relatively tasteless. Regardless, it is still viewed by many as a delicacy and there are rumors that it improves the health of the consumer. The high mercury content of shark fins is, of course, not mentioned in this sales pitch.[3]

The process in which their fins are obtained is merciless. Sharks, captured from their homes, are pulled aboard a boat to have all of their fins cut off and are then thrown back into the water still alive. They then sink to the bottom of the ocean floor, paralyzed, and slowly die. Many who are even unintentionally caught are assaulted in this manner due to the high price of their fins. Some countries have laws against this practice, but these laws are often not enforced. Annually, it is estimated that 20 million Blue sharks are killed for their fins.[3]

Where large shark populations were once abundant, many of their species have faced a steep drop in numbers. Overfishing is a major cause of this decline, as sharks are often caught alongside the intended target. Human decimation of ocean wildlife is detrimental for the actual carnivores who live there. As fish populations decline, as do their natural predators who suddenly struggle to feed themselves. Industrial fishing and animal agriculture in general have caused mass amounts of plastic & chemical pollution in the ocean which is constantly destroying habitats, trapping sea life and endangering our oceans.

Lobsters

Lobsters experience the world in a way that is only imaginable to most people. They have sensory hairs along their legs that they use to taste and their sense of smell comes from their antennas detecting various chemicals. Similar to us, Lobsters carry their young for 9 months and can live to be 100 years old. Unfortunately, many do not make it that long against their top predator: humans. In the United States alone, tens of millions of these creatures are consumed every year. Lobsters can migrate up to 100 miles a year in search for their ideal environment. Humans set millions of traps along the seafloor that capture them as they travel.[1]

Like all animals, Lobsters feel pain. In fact, it may even be a bit more intense than ours is. According to invertebrate zoologist Jaren G. Horsley, "The lobster does not have an autonomic nervous system that puts it into a state of shock when it is harmed."[1]

With this in mind, it's quite tragic that one of the most common methods of killing them includes conscious dismemberment and boiling them alive. When placed in the scalding water, their bodies twist and turn as they try desperately to escape the hell they've been placed into. Crabs are often killed in the same vicious manner.

Cows

Baby Watson, who resides at Iowa Farm Sanctuary

Personally, cows are some of my favorite animals. They are extremely gentle, cautious, loving and friendly. They have a sense of smell so strong that they can detect odors from up to 5 miles away. Their ears can pick up both lower and higher frequencies than we are able to detect and they have panoramic vision. Across the world, there are about 920 different breeds of cows. Mother cows form strong bonds with their children and when given the chance will sometimes nurse them for up to three years. They are social animals that form friendships with one another and will avoid those they dislike.[1]

As you are probably well aware, across the world these gentle giants are brutalized. They're mainly used for their flesh, milk, skin and in rodeos. Before we get into the nasty details, let's get one thing straight: the dairy industry is the meat industry. In the U.S alone, over 39 million cows are killed in the meat and dairy industries. Four companies (Tyson, National Beef, JBS Swift & Cargill) slaughter 80% of the cows in the United States.[2] In 2016, 300 million cows were killed globally.[3]

Cows raised for their flesh are typically kept in confined feeding operations where they may be dehorned, castrated and branded without painkillers. Many cows spend their first 6 months of life on a pasture. They're the ones you see grazing in fenced-in fields along highways. The Cow-calf operation is the first "stage of beef production" and often occurs on these types of farms. Mother cows generally give birth in the late winter. Branding, vaccinations and castration occurs in April for the calves. Then in the early summer, the cows are artificially inseminated (again). By October, calves are torn from their mothers in a process called "weaning."

Weaned calves generally go right to the sale barn, where they're auctioned off by the pound to feed lots. Nearly every cow raised for their flesh spends the last 6 months of their life in a feedlot, simply because it can make or break if a farmer will make a couple extra bucks on them. Cows used to be about 4-5 years old before being slaughtered, now they reach the desired weight of about 1,200 pounds at 14-16 months. This does not occur naturally, it is due to an intensive diet mainly consisting of corn, soy & hormones.[4]

This diet can actually kill their sensitive stomachs if not accompanied heavily with antibiotics. This is why cows are often pasture raised the first half of their short life, because if they were fed feed-lot diets their whole lives it's possible their liver would explode. The food fed to them is deeply unnatural, with additives such as feather meal & chicken manure being put into the food sometimes. Feedlot bloat is the most deadly occurrence from this dietary switch. A cow's rumen is constantly producing gas, which is normally released during rumination. However, a diet heavy in starch halts this process, causing a layer of slime to develop and prevent the gas from releasing. The rumen inflates and the cow can suffocate to death. This is precisely why after 6 months they're sent to slaughter.

How much profit do you think they make with each life they auction off ? $100 ? $200 ? $500? $1,000? A life surely couldn't be worth less than that... right?

" According to Cattlefax, a market research firm, the return on an animal coming out of feedlot has averaged just $3 per head the last twenty years."[4]

Astonishing.

Diving deeper into this industry, let's look into the process of artificial insemination. Male cows are typically bred for their flesh and their semen, but only the "best" bull is chosen for that role. Those deemed fit will be masturbated by a human who uses their hands, a machine, or they will electrocute their balls until they ejaculate. They then use this sperm to artificially inseminate the female cows on what the industry calls a " rape rack."[5] It's exactly what it sounds like.

Practically all female cows are sent to dairies to have their reproductive systems exploited. They are forcibly impregnated starting at the young age of two. They will have a 9 month pregnancy and begin producing milk for their baby. Once giving birth, their baby is stolen from them. Sometimes this is done immediately. Often it is within 24-48 hours of giving birth. Mother cows are known to grieve for days. They will cry, mourn and even search for their stolen babies, sometimes chasing the trucks that take them away.[6]

Now that the farmer has removed her baby and sent them to live in confinement with other stolen youth, they can steal the mother cows milk. She will be hooked up to a milking machine on average two times a day. Monsanto, the same company spraying poisons on our plants, is also responsible for producing something called recombinant bovine growth hormone (rBGH) which spikes milk production.[7] Not all farmers use this, but it's definitely not an uncommon practice in the US, especially when the ultimate goal is profit. This is also why, in order to make sure her milk supply is steady, she will be impregnated once a year and have to repeat the traumatizing process again and again and again. Cows can live an average of 20-25 years. However, in the dairy industry, mothers only make it to about 4-6, often due to illness. At this point, when they are no longer deemed profitable, they are sent to slaughter.[6]

"Each year 20% of dairy cows develop severe calcium deficiency, which if untreated can lead to death or mastitis, an inflammation of udder tissue by coliform bacteria, which can thrive in even the cleanest of dairies... untreatable mastitis infections and other udder problems have become so pervasive in the United States that they are responsible for sending nearly a quarter of dairy cows to slaughter each year."[7]

Let's take a look at what has happened to their babies in this time period. If the calf was female then she will be sent to a facility where she will most likely be chained or fenced into a little hut for the first several months of her life. She will be fed artificial milk and when she's old enough she'll suffer the same fate as her mother. Males, on the other hand, are often immediately murdered or sent to be raised for veal (baby cow meat). Sometimes, they are raised to adulthood and then later killed.[8]

In order to gather information for this book, I read the entirety of the book CAFO: Concentrated Animal Feeding Operation. In it, on page 152 the term "humanely raised pasture veal" can be found.[7] This is infuriating to me, because it implies that there is a benevolent or compassionate way to steal a child from their mother, raise them elsewhere and then slaughter them in their infancy. I honestly find it hard to imagine a crime so deeply harmful.

You may be wondering, "What about small, local, organic farms"?

Organic means practically nothing regarding animal treatment, it largely concerns the food they are being fed. Local doesn't mean ethical. Any farm is local to someone. Let me say that again, all Factory farms are local farms to someone. But, let's entertain the idea that local farms are "more" ethical because I have a personal anecdote I'd like to share.

When I first toured MIU I was told about this "wonderful" dairy farm they use called Radiance Dairy. People spoke of this place as if it was a sanctuary, stating that they don't kill their cows and they get to keep their babies and that they play music for the cows and it's all organic and wonderful. This felt way too fanciful to be the truth, so I asked for a tour of the farm.

While conditions on this farm, comparatively to factory operations, were better... they certainly weren't good. The cows wore collars with numbers on them and they were skittish around humans. The milking room was full of machines that looked quite unpleasant. They are artificially inseminated yearly and once the baby is born they "allow" them to stay with their mother for up to four months to bond, then they are kidnapped. If the cows live to be over 10 then they get to retire on a different farm, but if they prove to be unprofitable before then, and I quote the farmer here, " they become McDonald's."

Better than the worst still isn't good. The dairy and meat industry is riddled with the worst crimes we can imagine being committed against humans, yet we accept this violence as normal for other species every day. Now, let's take a look at the effect this is having on the oppressors (humans) for a moment.

With approximately 9 million dairy cows in the U.S. alone, each drinking about 12,000 gallons of water annually (this is a very low estimate that also does not include water used for feed, cleaning, transportation, etc.), then about 108 billion gallons of water are consumed by cows used in the dairy industry every year. Worldwide, there are about 264 million dairy cows at any given moment. Every year these cows directly drink over 3 trillion gallons of water.[9] In comparison, when considering the same factors, one human will consume about 365 gallons of water a year (high estimate).

Right now, about 1 in 3 people worldwide lack access to clean drinking water.[10] Next to many of these areas facing water insecurity are dairy farms in which the cows will never face the worry of not having enough food or water for the duration of their enslavement. Often, their flesh and secretions are sent to the western world for consumption.

If we were to stop forcibly breeding dairy cows into existence and wasting over 3 trillion gallons of water every year just for their consumption then we could drastically change the climate regarding water insecurity. We have more than enough water and food to nourish our population without exploiting others.

If you would like to look into how these methods of farming are harming the environment, please watch the documentary Cowspiracy on Netflix or YouTube. I will also be discussing it further in later chapters.

In addition to being used for consumption, cows are also used for entertainment, mainly in the rodeo or for bullfighting. I'm not going to go in depth regarding bullfighting here because of how uncommon the practice is, but if you'd like to see a watered down version of it then watch the children's movie Ferdinand. What I am going to speak about is the rodeo.

Common injuries for the cows & horses used at Rodeos include broken backs, tails, legs and necks, punctured lungs, internal organ damage and death. These damages occur in practice sessions as well. For example, a calf may be roped multiple times until their injuries are too impactful and a replacement victim is brought in. Often 2-3 cows are cycled through a single practice session. Many die in the practice arena[11]

In the actual event, calf's are tormented inside the pens before being released. Their tails will likely be twisted and they'll be shocked with metal prods up until the gate opens. At this point, they burst out of the pen to avoid the torment and are instead met with a rope around the neck snapping them to the ground. This act alone kills many calf's. (Interesting how grown men are viewed as tough by American society when they harass and murder baby animals. What does that say about our society?)

The animals used in these shows, specifically cows, are naturally peaceful beings. In order to force them into fear-based behaviors, they use tools of terror. An example of this is an electric prod known as a "hot shot". This is used on both the calf's and full grown cows. Straps with spikes are often fastened tightly around bulls stomachs and their groin area to make them buck in an attempt to get it off. For bull riding in particular, if the "sport" doesn't kill them then they'll be sent to slaughter once they're deemed unusable.[11]

Doctor C.G. Habor, a veterinarian who has worked for 30 years as a USDA Meat inspector, stated that: "The rodeo folks send their animals to the packing houses where...I have seen cattle so extensively bruised that the only areas in which the skin was attached was the head, neck, legs, and belly. I have seen animals with six to eight ribs broken from the spine and at times puncturing the lungs. I have seen as much as two and three gallons of free blood accumulated under the detached skin."[12]

There are many more horrific practices in the rodeo that I'm not going to touch on here; however, I strongly suggest looking at the page sourced below from the Humane Society Veterinary Medical Association to learn more.[11]

With all of the above in mind, I would like to remind you that virtually all cows who are raised in factory farms, in grassy fields and in the entertainment industry all go to the same place to die. And that place is absolutely horrific. I've seen trucks filled with well over 30 cows enter the gates of a slaughterhouse followed by a small trailer holding just one friendly cow. Feeding and looking after someone does not give us the right to take their life away from them when it is convenient for us. The ride to the slaughterhouse can be short, as some cows live right across the street from one and are forced to smell the blood of their kin constantly. Other journeys are much longer.

Sometimes, cows are shipped overseas to be slaughtered. This process is horrendous for animals, as the waves rock the ship and their captives back and forth relentlessly, and those who die or are severely ill are generally thrown overboard. Recently, a ship left from Spain headed to Turkey with 1,789 cows aboard. When they arrived at their destination, the captain was told that they were not allowed to disembark because they may contain a virus. The ship then spent three months wandering trying to find a place to unload and eventually ended up back in Spain. At this point, 179 cows had died. The rest were in unimaginable conditions. They lived on top of piles of their own feces and the bodies of those who had not been thrown into the sea. Many of the animals were unable to lay down in the crowded and disgusting conditions. A quarter of them had skin injuries, others had broken horns or tails. All of the survivors on the ship were then murdered.[13]

Arlo the cow, resident at Iowa Farm Sanctuary

Goats

Beth, resident at Iowa Farm Sanctuary

In their natural environment, goats live in social herds, roaming around mountain grasslands and enjoying their freedom. Goats are playful, inquisitive and highly intelligent. They love to explore and closely investigate anything new to them. Their coordination is remarkable, allowing them to scale cliff sides and even climb trees![1]

Goat mothers are known to be nurturing and attentive, which is why they're often chosen to foster abandoned calves and lambs. They can live to be 18 years old and form deep bonds with their young. Unfortunately, just like the cows in the dairy industry, mamma goats also have their kids and lives stolen from them. A piece of information that I found surprising is that a majority of the dairy consumed globally is actually produced by goats. While being fairly unpopular in the U.S, goat flesh is the most consumed red meat in the world. Raised for their flesh and their milk, just like cows, 450 million goats were slaughtered in 2016.[2] The manner in which they are treated is largely the same. Due to this, I will not be going into detail here since you've already read about these practices.

If you would like a visual image of what the standard industry practice of goat farming looks like: please watch the video on YouTube " Goat Milk - The Ethical Alternative?" By EarthlingEd[3]

Several months ago, my partner and I participated in an emergency hen rescue that I'll discuss in later chapters. We drove them to Broken Shovel Farm Sanctuary in Colorado. The sanctuary owner, Andrea, shared her story with us. Now, I'd like to share it with you.

Formerly, this sanctuary was a goat dairy. She was convinced that she could run an ethical dairy and worked very hard to make that a reality. She didn't do any of the standard procedures, like disbudding (searing a kid's horns off) or castration (cutting off a goat's balls, typically done with a tight rubber band). She was instead kind to the goats, refused to send them to slaughter, and adopted the kids to good homes.

What she learned was that there is not an ethical way to separate families against their will and take what is not yours. The mothers would grieve for days, crying out and searching for their kids. Watching them go through this process because of her actions was unbearable, so she transformed her farm into a sanctuary. She kept all of the goats she had and stopped exploiting them for profit. Her sanctuary now has over 500 animals, with about half of them being goats. She is a true example of aligning your actions with your ethics.[4]

Cheyanne & a goat (name unknown) who lives at Harmony Farm Sanctuary

Pigs

Bruce & Ginger, residents at Iowa Farm Sanctuary

Of the most common animals humans farm for food, pigs are some of the smartest by our scale of measurement. They have displayed cognitive capabilities that surpass those of dogs and of three year old children. They form close friendships, often with other species, and are extremely protective of their young. They are relatively peaceful animals and keep themselves and their spaces clean when given the chance.[1] This makes the horrific manner in which they are treated and confined, which they are extremely conscious of, to be incomprehensible.

Pigs enjoy rooting in the ground and finding their own food, which they have preferences for. In the industry, they are fed the same shitty food on an automated system day in and day out. Unfortunately, many are literally fed trash, plastic specifically. Bags of bread and other stale foods wrapped fully in the plastic are heated up to high temperatures and turned into a sort of brown dust, which is added to pig feed. These micro plastics get into their bloodstream and flesh, and end up in those who consume them.[2]

On any given day, there are around 71 million pigs in factory farms while over 161 million are slaughtered every year in the U.S alone.[3] The images of pigs running around in pastures and playing in the grass is really only a reality in sanctuaries. Virtually every animal sold for their flesh was raised in extreme confinement conditions, and if they were not, then they faced the ultimate betrayal as their caretaker sent them to slaughter.

Captive pigs in a CAFO in Iowa

Around 6 million of these pigs in captivity are mother sows, who spent nearly their entire life in gestation crates. The dimensions of these cells are typically 7 feet long and 2 feet wide - meaning they cannot even turn around. It's one of the worst types of confinement imaginable. After being artificially inseminated, carrying her young for several months and giving birth, then she will be moved to a slightly larger cell called a farrowing crate, which gives her just enough room to lay down and nurse her piglets, who are separated from her by metal bars.[3]

She will get the "luxury" of spending as little as 10 days with her babies before the survivors are taken away. She is then impregnated again and forced to repeat the vicious cycle again. Pigs can naturally live to be in their teens, but in this industry mothers survive to be only about 3-4 years old before they are then sold for their flesh after having been abused for the entire duration of their lives. Those who are being used solely for their flesh will be raised in a CAFO for about 6 months until they reach "slaughter weight". Then, the industry likes to refer to them as "hogs," and they are trucked off to a slaughterhouse. "According to industry reports, more than 1 million pigs die en route to the slaughterhouse every year."[3] During the stressful trip, they are denied food and water and arrive at the slaughterhouse extremely distressed.

Before describing what this process entails, I'd like to offer a perspective of what life could look like for these animals. A "pig park" was created by researchers from the University of Edinburgh in order to study the natural behaviors of pigs. They took pigs who would have usually been raised in confinement and instead released them in this make-shift natural environment for observation. To Quote an article by Bernard E. Rollin in the book CAFO, " In this environment, the sows covered almost a mile a day in foraging, and, in keeping up with their reputation as clean animals, they built carefully constructed nests on a hillside so that urine and feces ran downhill. They took turns minding each other's piglets so that each sow could forage. All of this natural behavior is inexpressible in confinement."[4]

The process of slaughtering these animals is disgraceful. In America, an average of 355,000 pigs are slaughtered daily. The typical slaughter rate of pigs is 1,000 an hour.[3] Line speeds are quick, workers, monotonously performing the same cold blooded actions over and over again, are desensitized to the violence while the stench of blood and feces is so thick that you can smell it from the streets. If a pig becomes too ill to make it to the slaughterhouse, workers will shoot them up with as many drugs as necessary to make them ambulatory. As long as they can walk themselves to the kill floor, they can be legally slaughtered and sold for their flesh.

There are two primary methods of killing pigs. The first involves using a stun gun, a knife and a scalding bath of hot water & the second involves a CO2 gas chamber. To Quote Matthew Scully's article in the book CAFO: " All these creatures, and billions more across the earth, go to their deaths knowing nothing of life, and nothing of man, except the foul, tortured existence of the factory farm, having never been outdoors."[5]

Recently in Iowa there was a newfound problem for pig farmers... Most slaughterhouses had shut down and they had nowhere to send the hogs at slaughter-ready weight. COVID-19 hit Iowa most significantly in the animal agriculture sector - particularly in meatpacking plants and slaughterhouses. This forced the factories, who had literally hundreds of employees test positive for the virus, to either limit operations or shut down completely until a solution came about. This presented a crisis for those who intended to send animals to be killed at these facilities.

Many farms elected to mass kill all of the pigs on site and then bury or burn their bodies... seriously. That's what they did. A method called Ventilation Shut Down was revived and enacted by major corporations. Iowa Select Farms (Iowa's largest pig killing company) was a particularly big culprit. An employee at ISF actually reached out to the animal rights organization Direct Action Everywhere to blow the whistle on what was happening because he was so horrified. An investigative team formed and they were able to get the first footage ever recorded of ventilation shut down.

Here's what they found:

They prepare a specific facility for the massacre, then they unload thousands of pigs into the shed. All airways are sealed off and scolding hot steam is pumped into the building. Over the course of several hours, the pigs are essentially slowly boiled alive while suffocating. The process continues overnight until most of the pigs are dead. The next morning, workers walked through the sea of bodies searching for signs of life from any of the victims. Some were visibly still breathing, still suffering, so they shot them in the head.[6]

According to the depopulation guidelines put forth by American Veterinary Medical Association, " The POD recommends that VSD only be used in facilities with the capability to adequately increase air temperature to a level that causes the generation of latent heat that results in a > 95% death rate in < 1 hour. The goal of any depopulation is 100% mortality, and this remains true for VSD."[8] Based on the footage and audio recording obtained by DXE, 100% mortality was certainly not achieved, even after a 12 hour period. It is also highly likely that a few of the pigs appeared dead, but were actually unconscious, in which case they were then buried or burned alive. ISF was crudely unable to meet the cruel standards that their very industry put forth for them.

ISF has since stopped doing ventilation shut down. This announcement came following a series of actions by DxE, involving activists (including myself & my partner) chaining themselves to the fence of a farm that was about to bring in pigs for VSD, releasing the video footage obtained, rescuing a piglet and burying dead piglets on the home property of the ISF's CEO - Jeff Hansen. Three days before my trial, I requested we subpoena a representative for ISF, to show them and the court what it was we were protesting and demanding justice for these animals. When ISF received the subpoena, *they dropped the charges against me.*

Activism works.

It also, unfortunately, encouraged the passing of a new law, House File 775. "Under the bill, knowingly entering private property without the owner's consent and taking soil and water samples or samples of an animal's bodily fluids or other animal products would become an aggravated misdemeanor on the first offense. That crime carries a sentence of up to two years in prison. A second offense would be a Class D felony, punishable by up to five years in prison."[9] This has obviously made the work we do much more difficult, making the footage and information we have already obtained that much more important.

To gain an understanding of the perspective of pigs on these farms I highly recommend watching this video by Direct Action Everywhere on YouTube: "Unseen – A look into the final hours of life for pigs from Smithfield"[7]

Dead pig on the loading doc of a CAFO in Iowa

Chickens

Injured chickens at the site of an overturned transport truck in Washington

Presently, there are around 23 billion chickens on this planet - nearly 3x the human population.[1] Every year in the US approximately 9 billion chickens are slaughtered. A shocking reality is that if you were to combine the number of chickens and turkeys killed annually in the US, it would account for about 99% of the land animals killed here.[2] This massacre is often justified with a baseless argument of intelligence, or lack thereof. There is an absurd idea that these animals are remarkably unintelligent; however, this couldn't be further from the truth. Numerous research studies have found that chickens, even newly hatched chicks, can count, show basic arithmetic and the ability to manipulate situations. On their first few days of life they outsmart even our newborns.[3] They also show signs of self-awareness and empathy among their kind. They have notable personalities, food preferences and some enjoy perching on the shoulders of humans.

What is interesting, is how humans assert that if someone is less intelligent than them then they are subject to oppression. Does this logic apply to young children, who have neurological capacities still developing ? What about our elderly folks who have dementia? What about those who experience severe brain damage? Do "lesser" cognitive functioning capacities really justify abuse? Even if chickens were "stupid," does that justify causing them unnecessary harm?

Think about that.

The exploitation of chickens can be categorized largely into two groups: Egg-laying and broiler hens. That is, hens used for egg production and those used for their flesh. We will be discussing the latter first. The image above is from an incident in my hometown of Battle Ground, Washington. A truck, carrying thousands of broiler hens, was headed to the slaughterhouse when they decided to make an illegal U-turn, which resulted in the truck tipping over. Many of the birds died on impact, while others were able to escape their now open cages and stumbled around confused and injured in a grassy ditch.

A dozen activists gathered and attempted to plead with the police, slaughterhouse, and factory farm owner to release some of them to us. Hours passed by without any success. We watched workers, who the slaughterhouse later stated were certified in "humane handling", grab hens by their legs and throw them into crates. Horrified, we watched on top of a small hill with the hens beneath us. We strategized - trying to figure out what the best thing to do was. No one felt okay standing by and doing nothing, but we also knew that if we grabbed birds and ran then we'd all get arrested and most likely be unable to save anyone.

As we were all still mulling over the limited possibilities, a hen started making her way up the hill towards us. No one had noticed yet. I started slowly making my way down, using my body as a shield to block her from the manager who had rough housed us earlier. He looked over and saw her making an escape. I stepped in front of her to block him, and as I did so, one of the other activists scooped up the hen and declared that she was going to take her to get medical treatment. An hour-long stand-off between Amber, cradling the hen, and the police ensued. Eventually, they ripped the hen away from her and she was arrested. Everyone went home that night devastated.

Fortunately, after all of the activity had cleared, some activists returned to the scene and found two hens who had evaded capture by means I will not be sharing here in case this situation happens again. They were able to rescue them, take them to a vet and bring them to a sanctuary that provided them with a safe home for the rest of their lives.

rescued hen from transport truck crash getting veterinary care

These two were able to experience the sun, grass and love, but they died a couple months afterwards. These types of hens have been genetically manipulated, beginning in the 1950s, to grow as big as physically possible in a very short amount of time. The hens in these photos are only six weeks old. They grow from a tiny chick to a massive bird in just six short weeks. Previous to genetic modification, hens took 15 weeks to reach "slaughter" weight.[4] Hens breast size nowadays is 80 percent more than it used to be. This is the opposite of natural, it's the product of un-ethically founded science that has made its way into our "food" systems.

Since the natural order has been manipulated so harshly, further measures are taken in order to ensure the hens have the best chances of making it to slaughter alive, since that's the only way they can make money off of them. Their methods of doing so have a detrimental impact on not only the hens, but for those who consume them & the environment. " As of 2006, nearly 70 percent of the 9 billion broiler chickens raised each year in the United States were legally fed small amounts of an arsenic compound — a suspected human carcinogen — as a growth promoter and to fight parasites. Traces of arsenic can end up in the chicken itself, as well as in the manure, which can decompose in the soil or run off in waterways, or the manure can re enter the food chain as a cattle feed supplement."[5]

Pumped up on drugs just to stay alive long enough to die in a profitable manner, hens experience a living hell on earth. The rapid growth of these hens makes basic tasks, such as moving from one place to another, difficult. By the time they get onto the transport truck, many of their bones will have broken from the enormous weight of their body. Often their organs give up under the crushing pressure around them. This whole experience is directly felt by these sensitive animals. They are in no way deserving of the suffering enforced upon them.

At the slaughterhouse, they are met with a brutal fate. They will be pulled by their feet out of the crates they were brought in and shackled upside down, fully conscious onto the kill line. The line speed at these death factories only appears to go faster every year - with the present rate being up to 140 chickens a minute. At most slaughterhouses they are first drug through electrified water that paralyzes them to a degree and makes it so that their feathers come off easier. Next they are led to an automated blade that slits their throat. Often there are workers nearby to kill those still moving. The birds are often frantically flapping around trying to free themselves during this process and sometimes miss the electric bath and/or blade. This unfortunately means that there are chickens who have entered this next process fully conscious, which former slaughterhouse worker Virgil Butler has reported. After the blade, their bodies enter a scalding tank of water, he stated that in this tank "the chickens scream, kick, and their eyeballs pop out of their heads."[2]

The term humane isn't even kind of applicable to this type of massacre. Another less common method of killing chickens that is typically done on smaller operations is called the Kill Cone. Here, chickens are shoved upside down into a long funnel and their throats are slit. They are fully conscious as they bleed out, blood pouring into their eyes and mouth while they desperately try to escape. Some larger operations use decompression tanks and gas chambers to execute masses of chickens. When you look on industry websites you'll see the phrase "humane handling," and "euthanasia" when they address these methods of destruction.[6] Euthanasia refers to a death given out of mercy, to someone who is chronically ill or on the verge of death. The word humane means "having or showing compassion or benevolence." Do you feel the way these animals are treated falls within these definitions?

Both hens rescued from the overturned transport truck

On the other side of chicken exploitation sit egg-laying hens. Modern egg farms hold tens of thousands of hens in layers of "battery" cages designed to collect their eggs. 130,000 hens can be in a single egg-laying facility while 30,000 broiler hens can be in a barn. In terms of the number of individuals and the length of their suffering, egg-laying hens are the most exploited land animals. " All but 5 percent of the 280 million hens in the US egg laying flock are raised in battery cages — typically made of wire and confining 5 to 10 birds."[5]

The life of an egg laying hen begins in a hatchery. Eggs are incubated for about 21 days on metal shelves. They emerge from their shells with their eyes open, fully aware of their surroundings. Here begins their first traumatizing experience. Sexing is the next step - in which workers will separate male and female chicks. In the egg industry, males are worthless. They do not lay eggs and they have not been genetically modified to grow as big as broilers, so their first day of life will be their last. After being sorted, most will be thrown onto a conveyor belt that will then dump them into a macerator, which will grind them up alive. Another common method of killing them is by dumping them into large trash bags, where they will slowly suffocate on top of one another. Other facilities use gas chambers. For every female born, a male is born. This equates to about 6 billion male chicks being killed annually for egg production.[7]

Females, whose reproductive systems will now be exploited for the rest of their lives, will generally have their beaks clipped, receive vaccines and be sent to a growing facility. (A not-so-fun fact is that a vast majority, about 70-80%, of all pharmaceutical drugs are given to animals to prevent them from dying "early" and to promote rapid growth.)[8] Debeaking is often done to the birds who will be sent to caged, free-range or organic barn farms. The purpose is to prevent them from severely injuring one another because that could cause economic loss for the f(h)armer.

The vaccinations for these animals are essential due to the way these animals are raised. An average of 12-20 vaccines are given to each chick to prevent deadly diseases from taking hold.[9] Some of these diseases are zoonotic. If you weren't before, then you may be familiar with this term now because of COVID-19. Zoonotic diseases are able to pass from non-human animals to humans. Factory farms are the perfect breeding ground for these diseases and the conditions in which they would be passed to humans. In fact, according to Doctor Benjamin Cuker, *"every known epidemic disease to plague humans originated in animals."* [10] If we want to avoid the next global pandemic, then we need to stop this barbaric practice.

I took the image above at a factory farm in Iowa. These hens have spent virtually their entire lives crammed inside a small cage with 8-10 other birds. Where many of them are sticking their heads out is where they receive their food. Their eggs fall below them and are collected daily. Water is delivered through a drip system. It's a highly depersonalized system of living. In a normal operation, the birds you see on the ground would not be there.

This day, however, was a very different kind of day in this barn. The owner of the farm put out a notification on Facebook that he would be killing all of the birds in this particular barn due to financial burdens (I believe this was the reason, it was never made clear to me). In his post, he said anyone could come and take as many hens as they wanted. Luckily, the activist community caught wind of this.

Within three hours of me telling my partner that I really wanted to rescue animals I was tagged in a post asking for someone to transport around 30 hens from that farm to Colorado (instant manifestation). We gladly accepted the opportunity and drove to the farm the following morning. It was my first time inside of this type of facility and it was absolutely horrific. The day before we arrived they had been taking hens out of cages and shoving them into CO_2 gas tanks right next to activists rescuing hens. Luckily, they weren't doing this when we were there.

Several farmer looking folks were there rounding up the hens. Many of the workers who were helping them move would grab as many as they could by their feet. One woman appeared to hold about 8 in her fist. They'd be harshly yanked out and thrown upside down. This would harm some of them physically. I remember one particular moment where a hen was screeching in the hands of this lady. I froze and every cell in me wanted to do something as the hen continued to cry out, but I knew I just had to keep rescuing as many birds as I could. We ended up getting 43 hens into the back of my partner's car.

Cheyanne holding a hen rescued from a factory egg farm in Iowa

They all appeared to be dehydrated and hungry, so we fed them lettuce during the nearly 12 hour drive to Colorado. I've never been in a car that smelled so bad, and I've also never been so happy to be in that kind of stench. These ladies experienced the sun for probably the first time in our arms. They were restless for a lot of the drive, however by the time night fell they all cuddled together in a big heap. They looked like a giant angel wing. When we arrived at their new home, we took them out one by one and brought them to safety. A good two days' effort on our part was quite literally life or death for them. I think what we need to remember, is how big of an impact we all have the capacity to make. Our actions truly do matter. They certainly did for these ladies.

Now, let's reflect on the egg industry a bit more. The hens you see above have been genetically modified to produce as many eggs as physically possible. Naturally, chickens lay around 12 eggs a year for breeding purposes. However, humans have manipulated them to lay anywhere between 250-300+ eggs a year.[7] This has a significant impact on their health, as laying an egg is a strenuous process on their body. Due to how many eggs they lay, many of the hens are calcium deficient and ⅓ will suffer a bone fracture before being killed.

To make matters worse, some farms starve the hens for a period of time because it's been shown that when they resume feeding they produce larger eggs.[11] The European Union has banned that particular practice. Hens generally only survive about 18 months in this industry before being sent to slaughter for not producing enough eggs.[7] Sometimes, instead of being hauled off to a slaughterhouse, they are buried alive or suffocate to death in CO_2 gas chambers. Many of them don't make it to that mark and die in cages alongside their cell mates. We witnessed this firsthand on that farm. A few birds in particular died with their heads hanging out of the cage, aching for freedom that their death finally gave them.

Now, you may agree that factory farming chickens is wrong, but what about free range, organic or backyard farms?

First and foremost, the males in the egg industry are still murdered, even if the females are sent to a farm that doesn't use all of the egregious practices we've gone over. This includes the chicks they sell at farmer stores. They're all coming from hatcheries, which are inherently based on the exploitation of the female reproductive system and the murder of males. On that note, it's important to take into consideration the will of the hens. Chickens lay eggs so that they can raise chicks. If a mate doesn't come along to make this possible, then they often eat their eggs to help them rebuild the nutrients lost in the production of making said eggs.

In this industry, mother hens never get to experience motherhood. It is constantly stolen from them and their children are almost always destined to have terrible lives. In nature, hens create nests and lay on their eggs to protect their young. They can even communicate with their hatchling through the shell separating them.[12] There's a reason humans use the term "mother hen" to describe a loving, caring mother figure.

Now, on the note of organic; all it means is that the hens are fed organic feed, not given antibiotics and have some access to the outdoors. Cage-free often just means they're all crammed into a barn together for the entirety of their life, which is just a large cage realistically. The industry definition of "free-range" just means having access to the outside for part of the day.[13] Sometimes, farms literally just have a small hole in the side of the building that some chickens make their way out of on occasion if they find it. And if they are truly free-range, in a large backyard per say, then we get back to the topic of motherhood. Chickens do not lay their eggs so that we can consume them. They did not consent to that, nor can they since they speak a different language. If you happen to have rescued egg-laying hens, then something that is helpful to do *if the eggs aren't fertilized,* is to feed some of them back to the hens so that they regain some much needed nutrients.[14]

Eggs are not an essential part of the human diet, and they're actually quite harmful for us. A study published in 2019, accounting for 30,000 adults over the course of 17 years, showed that for every half an egg a day consumed, the likelihood of the person developing heart disease rose by 6 percent and their risk of dying early increased by 8 percent.[15] Eggs are high in cholesterol levels, which is really only harmful for humans, since our body naturally creates all the cholesterol it needs. Furthermore, the FDA states that there are around 79,000 cases of food borne illness and 30 deaths each year in the US caused by eating eggs infected with salmonella.[16] Eggs also cannot legally be called healthy, safe or nutritious.[17]

All things considered, chickens are highly intelligent animals who outnumber us on this planet dramatically. Forcibly breeding them into existence for the pure purpose of exploitation is harmful, unnecessarily violent and unnatural.

Turkeys

Stratus, resident at Iowa Farm Sanctuary

Turkeys are social, intelligent and cautious animals. They are so sensitive to their own emotions that their heads will even change color! The more vibrant their color, the more intense the emotion is that they're feeling. Their head colors have the same theme of the American flag - red, white & blue. Perhaps that's why Benjamin Franklin felt they were respectable, true Americans.[1]

In nature, Turkeys navigate prairies and woodlands, often traveling in broods where the mothers team up to look after the groups young together. They have full color vision & its said that their eyesight is 3x better than our own.[1] Some of these birds are first able to take flight within their first two weeks of life, and at night they use this newfound ability to fly into trees and roost as a family.[2] This feeling of family, it seems, can be extended to humans, as well, once we have gained their trust. One time at Harmony Farm Sanctuary, one of the young men who ran the facility told my friend and I that he loved laying down and having the turkey's nest on his back. We were immediately intrigued and followed his lead. Soon enough, after circling us for quite some time and ensuring we weren't a threat, they nestled right on our backs. It's truly tragic that so few humans get to share this kind of loving interaction with these birds.

In the United States, 245 million turkeys are killed a year, 46 million of those for Thanksgiving.[3] Here in the U.S we kill over a third of the Turkey's killed globally - which is over 656,000 a year. In the U.S and most other nations, they have no federal legal protections and virtually all of them spend their entire lives on factory farms. For the vast majority raised on these farms, their life begins in an incubator. They will never meet their mothers and will live their lives in windowless sheds. At this stage of existence, part of their beaks, toenails and the males' snoods (the flap of skin under their chin) are cut off without pain killers to keep the birds from killing each other.[4] When in such crowded and maddening conditions, many of the birds develop violent and/or self-harming tendencies. This can be understood, when you imagine being crammed into a factory with up to 10,000 others for the entirety of your life.

Many will develop a stress related condition that causes them to stop eating. This, as well as, general unwellness common in these birds kills off some of them within the first few weeks of life. Like all other factory farmed animals, turkeys have been genetically manipulated since at least the 1960s. At that point in time, the "slaughter" weight for a turkey was 17 pounds, nowadays it is 30.[4] This has made it so that they're unable to reproduce naturally, so a vast majority of the turkeys alive today are via artificial insemination. Their enormous weight is crippling and many die of heart attack or organ failure before even reaching 6 months old. Around this time, those who have survived are trucked off to slaughter. They are killed in the same manner as chickens.

Pearson & Flower, Residents at Iowa Farm Sanctuary

Ducks & Geese

Activists locked down at a duck factory farm, hatchery & slaughterhouse in California

It's likely that you've seen ducks in their natural setting before. They are aquatic animals that spend most of their twenty year lifespan swimming in ponds, foraging for food and playing with their flocks. Cleanliness is important to most of them, and they have been known to keep their dwelling space tidy. They form lifelong friendships and migrate throughout the world in accordance with the seasons. In fact, they can be found on every continent except for Antarctica. Approximately 120 species of ducks are known of, and they are closely related to Geese & Swans.[1]

Geese live a similar lifestyle to ducks, with a more emphasis on romance. Geese mate for life and exhibit unwavering loyalty to their partner. Often, when their mate is injured or has died they will refuse to leave their side and will try to wake them up. Many have been observed to mourn their loss in seclusion and some will never mate again. They show similar behavior, with a bit less intensity, when losing their eggs as well. Not only are they protective of their immediate family, but they have been known to care for members of their flock who are injured or sick as well.[2]

All of these natural behaviors are stripped from them when crammed into dimly lit sheds by the thousands. Their natural order is in disarray and they go mad. They are typically given no access to swimming water which is dreadful for their water-bound bodies, and in most sheds the floor consists of a wire mesh to collect their feces beneath. This was the type of farm we were protesting in the photo above.

This particular farm was a hatchery, factory farm and slaughterhouse - all in one property. This means that these birds would quite literally never leave these grounds from birth to death unless they were rescued. Direct Action Everywhere conducted an investigation in which they found gross examples of animal abuse and neglect.[3] Due to the size these birds grow to and their less than life affirming conditions for living, many of them would collapse and be unable to get up to access food or water. They would then slowly starve to death. Evidence of this was found again in person when we infiltrated the farm. My team's responsibility was to block the gate with our bodies and chains. Another group found the pile of dead birds tossed out as trash and brought many of them to us so we could show the world the victims that these industries want forgotten. While we did so, another team rescued dozens of ducklings (who are now safe at sanctuary) and another team chained themselves to the slaughter line.[4]

As a group, our demand to the police was clear: start an animal cruelty investigation immediately and we will leave. Now, in most other states we would unfortunately have no legal backing to enforce this request; however in California we do. California Penal Code section 597e states, in summary, that if a person sees a domesticated animal being neglected food and water then that person may enter the property and supply that animal with necessary care. That person would not be subject to punishment for entry and could actually request compensation from the abuser for the costs of providing care to the animal.[5] Now, most states have a subsection that states something along the lines of " except for farmed animals" making it only really applicable to "pets". California does not have that section, and because of that a Harvard Law professor has written us a legal opinion stating that we are acting within our legal rights to take necessary action.

With this as our foundation, we took action. The police, who often protect corporations and not people, followed that trend. 80 of the 600 activists that day were arrested. The charges for most of them were dropped, except for those of us chained. We were originally arrested on felony charges and several misdemeanors, which got dropped to just "trespassing" very quickly. We originally intended to take the case to trial, then COVID-19 happened and our case got delayed two years. Per the advice of our legal team we agreed to take the deferment offered, which was essentially just a fine and 20 community service hours. I am happily serving my time at Iowa Farm Sanctuary.

Now, back to our main subject.

Ducks & Geese are killed for their flesh, organs and feathers. In the U.S, 27.5 million ducks were slaughtered in 2019.[6] This number does not include those who are shot in the wild for "sport." Many of those ducks are shot mid-flight and are actually never found by the hunter, causing them to slowly die from their injuries.

On factory farms, similar to other birds, ducks' upper beaks are often cut off to prevent them from pecking at their own feathers or one another due to stress. Humans, however, have no problem ripping feathers off of geese and ducks. A practice known as live-plucking is common to create "high-end" materials for down comforters, pillows and couches. Live plucking is exactly what it sounds like. Someone holds a bird down and rips out their feathers for long periods of time, then releases them back into the flock of traumatized birds. They then let the feathers grow back and repeat this process again and again, then slaughter the animals. It's a monstrous practice.

Roughly 80% of the world's Down comes from Chinese farms. Many farms claim to not use this practice anymore, but after an undercover investigation by PETA at 11 farms in China the evidence was clear that this practice is still alive.[7] This thorough investigation has led to several sellers looking more deeply into the farms they use to produce "ethical down," but the reality of "ethical down" is that it just means the birds are murdered before their feathers are ripped out of their dead body. Birds grow their feathers for themselves, not so we can pluck them for a jacket.

The production of Foie Gras, French for "fatty liver," is absolutely dreadful. It is known as a delicacy and a majority of it (75-80%) is produced in France. Here, ducks are kept in cages so small they cannot even extend their wings. Unlike most industries, only the males are used in this particular massacre. For these beings, their reality consists of being roughly force fed two to four times a day with a tube that pumps pounds of food into their stomachs. These pipes injure the birds sensitive throats, mouth and esophagus significantly. Their gag reflex is triggered every time they are force fed this way, making them convulse with every assault. This process alone kills many of the birds. The survivors live in a cage covered in vomit and spilled mush that coats their entire body. They are forced to live this way for 2-5 weeks before being killed for the "elite" to eat their livers. By this time, their liver has bloated to approximately twelve times its natural size.[8]

The process of being sent to slaughter for all of these birds is terrifying. At night, when the birds are naturally calmer, workers called "catchers" move through the sheds and grab birds, throwing them into crates. Once all the crates are full they are trucked off to slaughter. This ride will sometimes be the first time many of these birds have ever truly breathed fresh air, seen the stars or the sunshine (depending on time of day). Imagine if your only taste of the outside world was in your final moments of life.

Ducks are slaughtered in the same manner as turkeys and chickens. They are inverted (hung from their legs) on the slaughter line and dragged head first through an electric bath of water. This is meant to stun them for easier handling. Then they move onto an automated blade that slits their throat. Many of them are still fully awake during this and flail around, sometimes causing them to miss the blade. At this point, they will slowly drown to death in scalding hot water meant to defeather them.[9]

Sheep

name unknown, resident at Iowa Farm Sanctuary

Despite popular rhetoric, sheep are clever animals. A study in 2001 by Keith Kendrick found that sheep can recognize 50 individual faces for more than two years.[1] This outlasts the memory of many humans. In a different study, they showed the ability to navigate out of a maze and even quickened their pace when greeted by their fellow sheep at the exit. In addition to being smart, they form close bonds and long term friendships with one another. They are also quite the knowledgeable foragers. When they feel ill, they'll seek out plants to self-medicate with in order to feel better. They are joyful, playful and some have lifelong preferences of same-sex partners - about 8% of them in fact![2]

Prior to human intervention, sheep grew the perfect amount of wool to keep them protected from extreme weather temperatures. During the molting season, some people would pluck the wool naturally shedding from sheep. Then, shears were invented and everything changed. Humans began selectively breeding and keeping sheep for maximum wool production and stealing the thing that was supposed to protect these creatures.[3]

According to the United Nations, there are 1.2 billion sheep in the world. China is the biggest producer of sheep with around 200 million of them and Australia produces a quarter of the world's wool, having around 68 million sheep.[4] A general flock nowadays consists of thousands of sheep. This obviously makes it profitably impossible to give each sheep tender love and care before stealing from them. "During lambing season in Australia, between 10 to 15 million baby lambs die of starvation, neglect and exposure (often these are hypothermic deaths) within the first 48 hours of their lives."[5] To offset this financial loss for the f(h)armers, they breed them to produce more and more lambs.

The most common type of sheep raised in Australia is the merino, which is a breed known for their wrinkly skin. This is good for the industry because it means more wool. It's bad for the sheep because irresponsible shearers, who are typically paid by volume not by hour, rush to take all their wool and are more likely to injure the sheep. Aside from the cuts and open wounds caused by some shearing practices, under-cover footage has shown workers punching, kicking and standing on the throats of sheep. Some sheep die from this abuse.[6]

These wrinkly skinned sheep can also die of heat exhaustion in the summer due to their lack of proper insulation. On the other hand, they can die due to freezing temperatures if being shorn in the winter months. For those with wrinkles, often urine and moisture is trapped between the skin flaps, which attracts flies to lay eggs in them. When these eggs hatch they emerge as maggots that can eat the sheep alive.[7] A process known as Mulesing is done to try to prevent this, which is lit-erally carving large portions of their skin and flesh off their bodies. This process is obviously extremely painful for the animal. Mulesing is often done within the first 2-12 weeks of life, as are other painful procedures such as tail docking and castration.[3]

Once the survivors are no longer economically viable, they are sent to slaughter. This typically happens between the ages of 5-6. To put this into perspective, their natural lifespan generally ranges from 10-12 years old. As a whole, the wool industry is the meat industry. They are not mutually exclusive. Just like every other animal agriculture industry, sheep are forcibly impregnated so that the cycle of abuse may continue. Their babies may be used in the same manner as they were, or they may be killed prematurely so that humans can eat their legs and livers. Lambs, baby sheep, are often shorn before being slaughtered at just 6-8 months old. A majority of all sheep are killed before their first birthday.[8] Many of them then have to endure being jammed onto a ship and exported live overseas to the Middle East and North America for slaughter.

Horses

Horses used to run free on grassy plains with their families. They are nomadic grazers, and can spend up to 20 hours a day munching on grass. Wild horses live in herds of about a dozen. Mares, female horses, carry their young within them for 11 months before giving birth. In dangerous situations, the lead mare will direct the herd to safety while the head stallion (male) will stay behind to fight. Those who are hurt are protected by the herd and on average they can live to be 40 years old.[1]

While this may come as a surprise to many people, Horses are classified as livestock in the United States and many other nations. The history of horse exploitation is vast and expansive - ranging from warfare to agriculture to entertainment to transportation and food. Humans have eaten horses for thousands of years, and nowadays those who consume their flesh have begun calling it Chevaline. An article in the Atlantic titled "The Troubled History of Horse Meat in America" extensively discusses this complex subject. One piece of information I pulled from the article that is particularly disturbing is that "In 1997, the Los Angeles Times broke the news that 90 percent of the mustangs removed from the range by the Bureau of Land Management had been sold on for meat by their supposed adopters."[2]

To clarify, these are wild horses rounded up, captured and sold for slaughter. This was followed by an action from the Animal Liberation Front who burned down an Oregon horse Abattoir. It was never rebuilt and the activists were charged as terrorists. This was then followed by activists who took non-arsenistic approaches that eventually led to the Horse Slaughter Prevention Act.[2] In the United States, horses are still shipped off to be slaughtered in our neighboring countries of Canada and Mexico. Approximately 36,000 horses died as a result of this in 2020 alone.[3] In Europe, more than 100,000 horses are slaughtered every year for consumption and in Australia this number is around 30-40,000.[4]

In the United States, horses are commonly used for racing and riding. Before getting into horse racing, which is inherently cruel, I would like you to consider if you would be comfortable being someone's property, being taught to submit to them and allow them to put a ton of gear in your mouth and on top of you so that they may sit on your back while you trot around for a while. I, personally, would not be okay with this and I don't think that most horses are either. Horses are rode in peoples backyards, on trails, in rodeos and on racetracks. They are also used in the logging and other labor-intensive industries. While many don't see any issue with keeping a horse, caring for them and riding them, it really boils down to consent. Horses have virtually no way to consent to being ridden or owned. You can have a deep bond with a horse and care for them without getting on their back.

Now, let's get into racing. On average, 24 horses die every week in the US racetracks. PETA released a video called 'Horse Racing: Drugs and Death'[5] that clearly displays the violence in this industry. I highly recommend watching it. In this video, they reveal what was uncovered in a several month long investigation. The first human being investigated was Steve Asmussen - one of the most "successful" thoroughbred racehorse trainers. He also sports the most rule and drug violations of all major US horse trainers. The undercover investigator found that performance enhancing drugs were regularly given to these horses that allowed them to train through all of their injuries and pain. Some of their most prized horses had their hooves degraded to nubs from all of the labor forced upon them.

These horses, used purely for monetary gain, are treated as disposable commodities from birth to death. To this industry, that is all they are. They always have another horse, who has been forcibly bred into existence, to replace the last one who died. For many who are deemed no longer profitable, their existence will end in a slaughterhouse. To further the general abuse of this industry, Undocumented workers were used as labor for horse care. They were paid very little and some literally slept in the barns.

The process of being sent to slaughter is terrifying regardless of what your species may be. Horses are shipped or trucked to abattoirs for periods of 24+ hours without any food, water or proper rest. Many horses are injured and some die in this horrific journey. Horses are very skittish and untrusting of most humans for valid reason, making the process of stunning them difficult. Due to this many are struck several times in an attempt to render them unconscious, which often doesn't work at all. This means they are fully aware as they are bled out and dismembered. This is unfortunately the fate for many wild horses who have been caught, many horses who are unwanted former "pets," racehorses, and labor horses. "Kill" buyers often purchase horses off of Craigslist or auction houses to be shipped to slaughter.[3] It's common for the Amish community, who use horses to carry them around (you may even see them on highways in rural areas) and work in the fields, to ship them off to be killed when no longer useful.[6]

In rodeos, several horses have been documented snapping their spines and necks in the horrific events. Horses used for bucking often suffer tendon and bone problems in their legs, as well as severe back pain as it is not in their nature to move in such a manner. They are forced to buck the same way cows are, by tightening a strap around their flank which causes them to frantically try to get it off. In the wild, horses would buck when humans tried to domesticate them because they wanted nothing to do with us. Now, after generations of taming they have to force these horses to appear wild in order to entertain a crowd.[7]

Rabbits

Rabbits are social, intelligent animals who naturally live in forests, fields and nowadays, neighborhoods. They create long, complex underground burrows where they raise their young and escape to in case of danger. Due to their small size and relatively defenseless nature, they are acutely aware of any threats that may transpire. Often, they scope out a location they can flee to before grazing. Wild rabbits spend most of their life within the same 10 acre area, so they know it well! They can have several litters a year, with female rabbits being able to get pregnant again within four days of giving birth![1] Rabbits who have been domesticated are often affectionate and caring towards their human companions. In nature they live to be about 2 due to predators, but in the right environment they can live to be 10. Unfortunately, this often is not the case.

Rabbits are raised for their meat, fur, young and for laboratory use. A 2017 census of agriculture stated that 4,000 farms in the United States sold half a million rabbits nationally.[2] "The American Anti-Vivisection Society (AAVS) reports that in 2004, the number of laboratory rabbits in use was over 260,000, and some 43 percent of those individuals were subjected to tests that caused pain, distress, or both, sometimes without any drug relief."[3] These creatures are prime test subjects because of their small size and gentle nature. Drugs, chemicals and medical devices are commonly tested on rabbits. These tests can be extremely stressful,

harmful and sometimes deadly. Substances such as dishwashing deter-
gent are often dripped into their eyes which causes irritation displayed
in swelling, discharge and redness. They are kept in tiny cages and often
display signs of extreme stress such as self-mutilation, aggression, weight
loss and tremoring.[4]

The Humane Society of the United States reports that over 2 million
rabbits are raised in the United States annually for their flesh. They are
kept in cruel conditions similar to those of chickens - in tiny wire cages
that hurt their feet, crowded in with other rabbits and covered in their
own feces. They endure this existence for an average of 10-12 weeks for
White Rabbits 0r 8-9 months for Rex Rabbits before being trucked off
to slaughter, which is an absolutely brutal process. Rabbits are allowed
to be killed in quite literally any manner.[3] Since they aren't classified as
livestock, they are exempt from the Humane Methods of Slaughter Act
(none of these methods are actually humane - I may add.)[5] Methods of
murdering rabbits range from bludgeoning them with a steel pipe, slitting their throat and allowing them to bleed out, shooting them and de-
capitation.[3]

Globally, the United Nations reports that 1 billion rabbits are killed
for their fur.[6] Rabbit fur is primarily produced in Europe. France alone
produces 70 million rabbit pellets a year. The rabbits specifically bred for
their fur are Angoras, which are a different breed than those typically
used for meat or laboratory testing. Once they've reached a "mature" age
- about two months old - they will be stunned by a blow to the head.
Incisions are made in their skin then they are hung and bled out before
their fur is ripped off. The rabbits about to be slaughtered are able to
clearly see this entire process. Some rabbits have their fur pulled off of
their live body, which is an unimaginably painful process.[3]

Rabbits are the third most commonly euthanized companion animal.[7] Many people purchase rabbits as Easter presents or for children's birthdays. Once they are no longer desired they are often abandoned. Rabbits are bred by backyard breeders or rabbit mills. They are then sold in pet stores, carnivals and fairs. Proper education of how to care for a rabbit is almost never supplied. This leads to their mistreatment and death.

Foxes

Foxes are solitary animals in the same family as wolves and dogs. When they're young, they live in burrows with their families until they're grown. During their youth they are extremely vulnerable and rely on their parents for survival. The cubs are both blind & deaf at birth and take 11-14 days on average to first open their eyes.[1] Their mother stays with them in the den at this time and their father finds food for the family. They act as a family unit for six to seven months. During this time they are loyal to one another and are often very playful. They've been known to steal balls from golf courses to play with.[2] They are nocturnal animals, venturing out primarily after sunset. Foxes move similarly to cats and some love to climb trees, even sleeping in them sometimes.[3] They have sensitive whiskers, making them acutely aware of their environment. It's even been theorized that they use the earth's electromagnetic field to hunt.[4]

Foxes are routinely hunted for sport, killed for being a "nuisance" and raised for their fur. Sometimes award money is given to the hunter who has killed the most foxes. Dogs are used in this hunt as well. In "fox penning" packs of dogs are released to hunt foxes in a closed off area, meaning the foxes have literally no chance of escaping. They are chased to a point of absolute exhaustion then literally ripped apart.[5] Some brave activists sabotage these hunts to the best of their abilities.

Foxes raised for their fur are brutally murdered and confined throughout their life. Many nations have banned fur farming, but still import fur from countries who allow it. China and Poland are massive producers of fur.[6] A majority of the fur produced comes from factory farms. The way they are raised is similar to that of rabbits, in extremely close quarters with others in very small filthy cages that limit them from exhibiting any natural behavior. Foxes are typically raised for seven months before being electrocuted to death in order to not taint their fur. This is often done with an electric rod shoved in their anus.[7]

Mink

Minks generally live around lakes, streams or ponds with nearby forest cover. They make their homes in hollow logs or dig dens in the earth. They are known to add bedding to their dens with grass, leaves or fur from their prey. Similar to foxes, mink primarily live in solitary, coming together to mate and raise a family for a period of months.[1] When content, minks sometimes purr.[2]

Minks are primarily raised for their fur. In the United States, approximately 275 "small family farms" (as the industry calls them) produce 3 million mink fur pelt a year. Wisconsin produces a third of this total. According to Fur Commission USA "Today's farm-raised mink are among the world's best cared-for livestock. Good nutrition, comfortable housing and prompt veterinary care have resulted in livestock very well suited to the farm environment."[3] A video on that same page about the Zimbabwean mink farm shows what they deem as top tier quality. This video shows minks kept in tiny sheds, being fed ground up leftover animal flesh in a mush and being handled in a way that is clearly distressing for them.[4] They are talked about purely as commodities because that's what they are to them. The fact that this is their best standard is despicable. All of this for around $40 a pelt on average.[5]

Minks are semi-aquatic animals, but in the tiny cages they are kept in they never have the opportunity to swim. In some farms they're barely able to turn around, while in others they have enough room to pace around a bit. This type of living confinement for the entirety of their life can drive them insane - causing self mutilation and cannibalism. This is why they are often kept separate from other minks. At six months old, they are killed. Common methods of killing mink to preserve their fur include anal and oral electrocution, suffocation, skinning them alive and snapping their neck. This is information you won't find on fur industry pages that talk about how important animal welfare is to them. 50-60 mink are murdered to produce one mink coat.[6] Dozens of deaths for... fashion?

Rats & Mice

Rats & Mice are inquisitive, social animals who have shown care for their friends and bond to humans when given the chance. They've even been known to care for sick members of their group. Going beyond that, both species have displayed altruism — putting themselves in harm's way to save another.[1] They have a long lasting memory, problem-solving skills and can learn quickly. They are playful and even express a chirping sound similar to that of human laughter when being tickled. High-frequency sounds that humans cannot perceive are used as the primary form of communication between one another for these rodents. Our family used to care for a rat named Sarah and often we'd let her run around in certain rooms with us. If she disappeared, we would simply call her name and she'd come running, often scurrying up our legs to perch on our shoulders and give us little kisses. Sarah completely changed my perception of her species at the time.

Unfortunately, these beings are often seen as pests and disposable test subjects. They are often viewed as dirty animals, despite the fact that they clean themselves several times a day. People frequently lay out painful glue traps that cause an agonizing death for many who live in homes, while millions are bred for experimentation. According to Veterinarian Dr. Larry Carbone, who published an analysis in the journal Nature, an estimated 111 million rats and mice are used in laboratories in the United States alone every year.[2] This figure is hard to pin down due to the fact that US researches aren't required to keep track of how many mice/rats they kill, so it's possible that there are less or more than estimated.[3]

The quantity of mice & rats being used in labs is debated, however the fact that these animals make up a vast majority of all lab animals is not. Even with conservative estimates, these animals make up roughly 93% of all laboratory animals in the states, though they are exempt from the only animal welfare act designed to protect animals used in labs. They are typically caged in plastic containers the size of shoeboxes and used for literally any experiment you can think of and many more.[4] The scope of experiments performed on these animals are so extensive that novels could be written on them.

Being excluded from the Animal Welfare Act means that laboratories that exclusively test on mice & rats are completely free of federal inspection. There's an estimated 800 laboratories like this in the US.[1] They are allowed to do quite literally anything to these animals. And they do. Depending on the laboratory, they endure experiments such as having holes drilled into their skulls, undergoing spinal surgery, having hard drugs pumped into their system, being given tumors and other severe diseases.[1] Some are slowly poisoned to death and others are forced to do bizarre tasks that may end in their demise. The more I read about the experiments conducted on these beings the more I am able to envision what a living hell is.

Nonhuman Primates

Primates are an empathetic, highly intelligent group that includes a diverse range of 200 species - us included.[1] When kept in laboratories, zoos or at home as pets their needs are vastly unmet. While it is illegal to import nonhuman primates into the United States (it still happens though) it is perfectly legal for domestic breeders to sell these creatures to desiring humans. These breeders typically take the mothers baby away from her soon after birth, keep them in small cages and enforce painful procedures upon them to make them appear less dangerous, such as canine pulling.[2] They are then sold primarily online or through newspaper ads. Many look to use them as replacement children if they are infertile or as a status symbol. The typical prices can range between $1,500 - $50,000. Practically every species can be bought, including those that are endangered.[3]

There are likely fifteen thousand nonhuman primates kept as pets in the US, but truly the number is unknown since many are obtained through illegal methods and go unreported.[3] Nonhuman primates are incredibly social in nature with their kind, yet living captive in a house is devoid of any natural social interaction their biology is accustomed to. This leads to mental deterioration and anxieties. As they are wild animals, they often begin exhibiting these traits as they age and many people decide soon after infancy that they are no longer able to care for these animals. Only a few make it safely to sanctuaries. Some are sold to circuses or other humans who are likely to follow the irresponsible trend.

Those who do not originate from breeders were likely captured from the wild. In places where these animals are indigenous, locals looking to make income will often slaughter entire families to capture baby primates. The deceased family members are then sold for their flesh. An estimated 10 adults are killed and sold for their flesh for every infant captured. The illegal bushmeat trade in Africa poses the most serious threat to the great ape population there.[4] These species are slow to reproduce, so the globalization of this once small market has now pushed many of these species to the brink of extinction. In addition to hunting them for their flesh and children, deforestation for farming and products such as palm oil destroys the natural habitats of many of these animals.

In laboratories, these animals are treated as disposable objects. In the U.S about 108,000 primates are used in laboratories[5] and in the UK that number drops to 3,000.[6] These beings are either captured from the wild or bred in captivity before being subjected to cruel, painful and often deadly experiments. Their natural life of lush jungles is just a dream to those in lifeless steel cages. The conditions and torture they are subjected to is maddening. Like other animals confined in labs, they often exhibit behaviors such as rocking back and forth, self harm and endless pacing.

Primates are forced to undergo some of the most cruel tests imaginable. They are tested to determine the safety of pharmaceutical drugs by having thick tubes shoved up their nostrils or down their throats so that drugs can be pumped into their stomachs. This is enraging in itself, but when you factor in the fact that the National Institutes of Health states that nonhuman animal tests show a 95% failure rate at determining the safety and effectiveness of these drugs on human bodies, then the sanity of the humans running these experiments is truly questionable.[5] In addition to general drug tests, vaccines are tested on primates after they've been injected with an infectious disease. You can probably imagine how terribly this goes for the animal. Experimental brain surgeries, psychological torture and military training techniques are all more examples of horrific practices forced upon these animals.

In 2020, the scientific community began to face a "monkey shortage" due to COVID-19. While primates only represent about 0.5% of laboratory animals in the US, they are typically the final step until human trials begin. Virtually all primates that governmental bodies have their hands on are being subjected to vaccine trials that may end in their death as we speak. While there are three vaccines for COVID-19 in circulation currently, about 100 more have been developed.[7] This makes it an increasingly unsafe time to be a monkey used in biomedical research.

Another aspect of the primate industry that is less widely known is those being used in coconut farming. Thailand coconut farms specifically are responsible for a third of the world's coconut exports and have been found to use monkeys for a bulk of this labor. Pig-tailed macaques are taught to climb trees and pick coconuts for the company. When they're not working, they're often chained up or in cages so small that they cannot turn around. It's likely they were stolen from the wild for this purpose. A PETA investigation in 2019 found them screaming and pacing in their severe confinement. Many of them had their main form of self defense, their canines, removed. Edwin Weik, who serves as an animal welfare advisor for Thailand's parliament, estimates that around 3,000 monkeys are used for these purposes and that half were taken from the wild illegally.[2]

Dogs

Friendly dog that a team of activists rescued in Stockton, California

Dogs are often viewed as beloved family members. They are bright, kind, loyal and protective. Modern day dogs descended from wolves due to years of selective breeding and domestication from humans. Nowadays, we have dog breeds ranging from Pomeranians to Great Danes and beyond. They have an incredible sense of smell approximately 10,000 - 100,000x stronger than our own and can even sniff out medical problems, as well as, our emotions. Even though they're all born deaf, they develop a keen sense of hearing that is about 4x stronger than our own.[1] Their intelligence is compared to that of a two year old child due to their ability to remember and respond to over 100 words and gestures. I personally think they're much smarter than we give them credit for.

Unfortunately, these animals are often abused and used for their puppies, hunting, fashion, food, fighting, racing and service. Many of them spend years upon years in shelters waiting for a new family. The U.S. sees about 3.3 million dogs entering shelters a year, with about 390,000 being euthanized.[2] Many are not euthanized because they are aggressive or ill, but because the shelter gives them a certain amount of days to be adopted before being put to death. This is certainly not the case for all shelters. Many are well intentioned, and have a no-kill policy. To obtain this label, the shelter must be able to home 90% or more of their rescued animals. They are permitted to euthanize animals that are severely ill and deemed as untreatable.[3]

The dog in the above image was one of my three that myself and several other activists rescued in Stockton, California. They were in a small, concrete, fenced in space with broken glass on the ground, virtually no shelter, and filthy water. They were sweet and approached us at the fence, which is when we noticed they were absolutely covered in ticks. We were able to convince their caretaker to surrender them to us, and we found them a shelter that could clean them up and house them until they were adopted. They all have new homes now.

Often, like the case above, dogs are neglected by their human caretakers. Puppies are sometimes bought as presents and not realized to be the 8-20 year commitment that they are. Dogs are viewed by many to be disposable and when they are no longer desired they simply put up an ad for them to find a new home or in worse instances just abandon them on the side of a road. Sometimes, the people responding to these ads take in free dogs to use as bait in dog fights. Animals like rabbits and cats are used as well. Dogs trained to fight are often bred for the role and conditioned to be violent their entire life through abusive training methods. They will be taught to attack small dogs and other helpless animals as viciously as possible, then expected to show vigor in the ring. Dog fights typically last 1-2 hours and end when one of the dogs is unable to continue because they are either severely injured or dead.[4] Humans gather and bet on which dog will win the blood sport. In the United States, dog fights are a felony offense, which is certainly discouraging for those who organize and participate in them, but not enough to actually stop them from happening.

On another end of the "dogs raised to kill" spectrum, many dogs are specifically kept for the purpose of serving a job - such as hunting. Many people use dogs to fetch birds that were just shot, sniff out pheasants and to viciously tear up foxes or to attack and immobilize boars. They are often kept alone in backyards or in kennels until it is time for them to work. As mentioned before, their hearing is significantly stronger than ours. Most dogs understandably freak out over fireworks, yet they are desensitized to not react to actual gunfire with no ear protection. Many hunting dogs are underfed so that they perform "better" and in some places literally thousands of dogs are abandoned after hunting season comes to a close. A specific breed of dog, the galgos, are typically killed after one or two hunting seasons, with an estimated 100,000 murdered annually.[5] Reports in Spain even state that hunters have thrown their dogs in wells and even tied them to railroads.[6] Others just leave them in the woods to fend for themselves. This is certainly not the reality for all dogs used for hunting, but the notion of using someone to be an accomplice to murder and submit to you is deranged in and of itself.

Another horrific act that should be a crime is what occurs inside of laboratories to dogs. These animals actually used to be stolen and taken off of streets to be experimented on in labs. Some probably still are. This is what sparked the creation of the American Anti-Vivisection Society - where much of the information in this section is sourced from. In 2018, the USDA reports that 65,000 dogs were being held in laboratories across the states. Most of the dogs in labs nowadays are bred into existence to serve that dystopian purpose, but when the scientists aren't able to find their desired dog through a breeder, they seize them from shelters and pounds. Beagles are the most common dog used in these laboratories due to their size and relatively tame nature. The primary use of these animals is for biomedical research that often revolves around cancer, heart and lung diseases, as well as toxicity studies for drugs. These experiments are often painful, and their life in a lab is void from any loving connection or freedom.[7]

Greyhounds, who are able to reach speeds of 45 mph and sustain it for miles, are often used in races that have similar costs to that of horse racing. They are typically confined in "barren warehouse style kennels for up to 20 hours a day".[8] They are let out to train, relieve themselves and to race. Injuries sustained in racing can be significant and animals, such as live bunnies, are used as bait to encourage the animal to run around the track. The high injury rate in this blood sport creates a mentality in which the animals are disposable, since they're likely to die or get severely hurt anyways. Due to this, around 3,000 to 8,000 greyhounds are killed in the US alone because of racing. A veterinarian nurse in Australia recently blew the whistle on the Industry there, stating in an interview that "You get eight dogs dropped off, oftentimes they will be just

… absolutely bled to death and euthanized, put in a body bag and put in the freezer and taken away for incineration. That's absolutely routine. No one would bat an eyelid at that being the reality."[8]

Another way dogs are raced is in a popular event you are likely familiar with, the Iditarod. Dogs are selectively bred for the sport and trained intensively. Those who don't meet the standards put forth are often killed or abandoned. According to one Iditarod racer, they breed an average of 300 dogs to get 5 usable ones.[9] Several cases of severe neglect, such as starvation, untreated illness and death, have been documented by those who 'own' these animals. It's typically for a sled dogs 'home' to be a tiny sleeping shelter which they are attached to by a short chain. Their lives are often devoid of any true love or affection and they are sometimes left alone (aside from receiving food/water) for months at a time.

In 1991, Marilee Enge reported this in the Anchorage Daily News: "Iditarod musher Frank Winkler was charged Friday with animal cruelty for bludgeoning 14 sled-dog puppies with an ax handle, although he said in an interview earlier this month that he reluctantly shot them. After a neighbor reported hearing puppies whimpering in the night, an animal-control officer visited Winkler's trailer Sept. 7 and found the battered puppies piled in a crate in the back of his pickup. Two were barely alive and the rest were dead. One of the live pups 'was crying and was cold, clammy, wet, bloody and showed clinical signs of shock,' Assistant District Attorney Mindy McQueen wrote in a charging document. The other was half-buried in the pile of dead pups. Both live dogs had crushed skulls and were later killed by animal-control officers."[9]

The dog's wellbeing is not the priority for the people responsible for this abuse, it is profit. For these dogs, proper care only comes if they are rescued. Taking care of just one dog can be quite expensive, especially if they're sick. Now imagine what the cost would look like if you have a kennel of 200 dogs? 300? 500? These are actually how many dogs several of these mushers own. It's just not financially viable for those trying to profit off of these animals to keep them healthy and happy. It's much cheaper to just let a sick dog die. So that's what they do. In the negligent conditions they're in, it's quite easy to fall ill. They're often fed expired or rotting food, sometimes only being fed once a day, not given fresh water regularly and not given proper protection from the elements. One dog handler in the business reported that dead dogs were sometimes skinned for their fur then fed back to the other dogs. While their medical problems are often neglected, many do go through procedures that benefit humans, such as debarking them (making it so they can no longer bark) and cutting their canines so that they cannot attack their abusers.[9]

It is likely you are familiar with the term puppy mill. These operations are essentially factory farms for dog breeding and provide about 90% of dogs found in pet stores.[10] The animals here often spend their life in extreme confinement devoid of any love or proper care. While most people are against puppy mills due to years of successful protests, I'd like to address the core issue of breeding in general. There are people who claim to be ethical backyard breeders - which essentially just means it's a family or small operation doing the deed. Let's consider one thing for a moment - imagine being impregnated, often forcibly, carrying your young for several months and then giving birth. You spend the next several weeks bonding with your babies and then slowly one-by-one they are taken from you until none remain. Then, you are impregnated again and the cycle continues over and over again until you're no longer usable. This is the reality of basically any "breeder" animal. While puppy mills are horrific, breeding operations in general are a violation of the female reproductive system and are exploitative in nature.

In some countries around the world, mainly China, Vietnam, South Korea and Indonesia, dog meat is consumed.[11] There are dog farms that resemble puppy mills and thousands of dogs are taken from the streets to be killed and eaten. Some are stolen from backyards or purchased from their "owners." They are then crammed into tiny cages and trucked to a slaughterhouse where they will be beaten to death, hanged or sometimes boiled alive. About 20 million dogs are slaughtered annually in China and 5 million in Vietnam.[12] It's important to note that while dog meat consumption does occur, many people are against it. Just as bacon festivals in the U.S. draw in protestors, the Yulin Dog Meat festival does the same. Activists in these nations are constantly working to free and protect these animals.

Dogs do not exist to serve us.

Cats

Luna being a good girl

If you've ever met a cat, you're likely to know that most have clear boundaries that they will inform you of if you cross. I know that my kitty companion Luna (pictured above) will gladly let me know when I've pet her for too long. She's also happy to let me know when the sun is about to rise with meows and when her food bowl is less than 100% full. Luna loves to go outside, climb trees, roll in the dirt and then spend an hour cleaning herself. She adores cuddles and sitting at my feet in the bathroom. She also just loves hanging out. When I'm in the shower she likes to wait for me on the shower mat and when I come home she greets me. I fully recognize her distinct personality and her individual wants, needs and desires as a fully conscious Being whom I am happy to co-inhabit a home with. She is a little loaf of sunshine and darkness. Having her in my life is an absolute blessing and I wish all cats were viewed in this manner. To be fair, all cat's are not Luna, but they are all lovely in their own unique ways.

Cat's are known for their distinct personalities and emotional complexities. In fact, humans and cats share an identical region of the brain responsible for emotions. Cat's spend about $2/3$ of their everyday life sleeping. As someone who shares a home with a cat, I can attest to this. I often wonder what they do in the dream realm. When they are awake and active, they are incredibly agile. A healthy cat can run up to 31 mph and jump 5x their height. They often fall relatively gracefully and have even been recorded surviving a fall of 65 feet. Cat's are often considered to be beloved family members. They can be found in about 30% of all North American homes. In the U.S. they are the most common "pet", with about 73 million of them living in homes with humans.[1]

With that said, they do still undergo forms of abuse including household neglect, abandonment, laboratory experiments and breeding - to name a few. PETA's website states that:

> "More than 19,000 cats are abused in U.S. laboratories every year—in addition to the tens of thousands who are killed and sold to schools for cruel and crude classroom dissections."

An undercover PETA investigator, working within the University of Utah's laboratories, discovered that a "pound-seizure" law forced animal shelters to hand over hundreds of cats and dogs. These beings were used in painful experiments that often ended their lives. On PETA's website, they share some of what was witnessed:

"One pregnant cat who had been purchased from a local animal shelter for $15 gave birth to eight kittens the very day that she arrived at the university. A chemical was injected into the kittens' brains, and all the kittens died. In another experiment, a cat named Robert, who had also been bought from a local shelter, had a hole drilled into his skull and electrodes attached to his brain. Following PETA's vigorous campaign, the university announced that it would no longer obtain animals from shelters, effectively ending pound seizure in the state of Utah."[2]

At the University of Wisconsin-Madison, acts of literal terror are conducted. The horrific lengths that these experiments go to include, but are not limited to: drilling holes into cats skulls and implanting steel coils into their eyes, intentionally deafening and then killing them, blocking blood flow to their brains to force them into a stroke, and sewing their eyes shut. To read about these experiments more in depth, please visit peta.org.[2]

The abuse of cats is nothing new, and certainly doesn't end in the laboratory. Historically, cats have been demonized alongside witches. They are seen to be their companions, specifically black cats, and as the prejudice against witchcraft still runs thick, as does the ostracization of our feline friends. The practice of burning witches at the stake was expanded to their apparent familiars as well. In previous times, popes ordered the execution of any cats seen as a way to ward away the devil. Sometimes they were abused for the sake of music, having their hair ripped out so that their howls could be added to songs.[3]

Nowadays, the most common form of cat abuse is found on the streets and in our homes. An estimated 82 million cats live on the streets of the United States, with around 3.4 million entering shelters every year. Around 74% of all cats who enter shelters are euthanized for a variety of reasons, some of which simply include just not being desirable to humans. For feral cats, those who have not lived with humans, entering a shelter is a death sentence.[4] Humans see animals who aren't comfortable around us as being burdensome and dangerous, so we kill them. Cat breeders only add to the problem, as people often flock to them for a new kitten instead of a shelter.

The leading cause of death for cats is humans.

A more obscure practice includes killing cats for their flesh and fur. It's estimated that ten million cats are killed annually across Asia for this purpose.[5] Like dogs, they are often taken from the streets and peoples homes, stuffed into tiny cages with others of their kind and then brutally slaughtered. I would like to state that while this is obviously horrific, it is not objectively more cruel than killing and eating a cow, chicken, pig or rabbit.

Deer

Deer are cautious herbivores who often travel in small family units or herds. Depending on the region and local population, deer herds can grow to have 100,000 members. There are about 50 known species of deer spanning across every major continent aside from Antarctica. Each species of deer has a different set of characteristics and lifespan, but on average they can live to be 10-25 years old. Deer are both playful and peaceful and can make long lasting friendships with members of other species. They have an incredible sense of hearing and the ability to rotate their ears without moving their head. Their sense of smell is heightened as well to allow them to pick up on the scent of predators. Depending on the region, deer have a wide variety of natural predators including wolves, cougars, coyotes, black bears and alligators.[1] Due to the declining number of natural predators, humans are deer's biggest threat.

Around 6 million deer are killed by hunters and over 1 million by cars every year.[2] Hunters like to say that these creatures are "overpopulated" and that they must be killed off by humans to maintain a healthy ecosystem. I feel that the assumption that another group is either overpopulated or invasive is quite a bold statement coming from our species. With that said, who crowned us with the right to murder anyone we don't want around?

In the areas where deer are truly overpopulated it is because humans kill off all of their natural predators which then throws the ecosystem way out of whack. Any animals that are seen as a threat to humans — wolves, coyotes, foxes, bears, mountain lions — are hunted down and killed. Entire wolf packs are sometimes executed for the crime of existing. If the deer population in some regions is a problem then a simple solution would be to stop killing animals that would naturally hunt them.

The reality, though, is that a majority of those who hunt like to call it a sport. They enjoy it. Unlike actual predators who generally go for the weakest link of a herd, which preserves ideal genetics for futures to come, humans want the biggest antlers to hang on their walls so they go for the strongest male they can find. When being chased by a wolf pack, deer have some sort of a chance for survival. But when a human shoots them multiple times with a gun, they are relatively defenseless. Those who were shot, that do escape their killer's grasp often suffer immensely before slowly dying. It's a gross violation of natural order and tears families apart. There are videos easily found online of a baby deer desperately trying to wake up their mother who was just shot and killed by hunters now laughing at the infant's despair.

"Hunting is often called a sport as a way to pass off a cruel, needless killing spree as a socially acceptable, wholesome activity. However, sports involve competition between two consenting parties and the mediation of a referee. And no sport ends with the deliberate death of one unwilling participant."[3]

I would like to add that there are some instances, like Indigenous people who live off of the land, where hunting is actually done for necessity. Hunting because that's the only way you're able to survive the winter and hunting for fun on the weekends are two completely different things.

When you look at most indigenous beliefs, they're centered around the respect for life, death and the souls of all of earth's creations. This way of thinking differs greatly from the way most humans view other animals, and this is why we've gotten where we are now as a society.

In addition to hunting, one form of deer is facing wildlife extinction and is increasingly kept in captivity: reindeer. In the 48 continuous states, there are only 3 wild reindeer left, of which all three are female. In Canada, their last remaining herd has 4 members. For these herds, the loss of their natural habitat and the wrath of human hunters has been devastating.[4] For those who live in captivity, especially in the states, they are often kept alone in a small stall or shed and used as a holiday prop. Their primary natural behaviors, such as living a nomadic lifestyle within a herd, are taken away from them for human entertainment.

Wolves, Coyotes, Cougars & Bears

I've grouped these animals together because they are all killed off for being a "threat" to humans & their livelihood. USDA Wildlife Services, which is a government branch tasked specifically with killing wild animals, has massacred 1.5 million wild animals in 2020. The number of predators killed by this organization annually is estimated around 100,000.[1] Methods of murder range from aerial shooting to poison/gas to deadly traps and snares.[2] Several non-target animals such as endangered species and domesticated animals accidently detonate some of the traps left and die as well. These deaths are often hidden and blatantly lied about by the rogue government agency that is Wildlife Services. I will be going over each individual predator species briefly.

Wolves are pack animals that can live to be 13-16 years old and act as the genetic ancestors of all dogs. They are loyal to their alpha's and sometimes even stay by each other's sides if one of them is caught in a snare. They are what's known as a keystone species, meaning their existence is vital for the ecosystem they live in. They typically hunt animals who are sick, injured or weak which preserves the strongest genetics for the deer, elk or bison they hunt. Their leftovers feed other predators such as coyotes, bears, eagles and crows.[3] The effects of their importance was viewed directly in Yellowstone national park when they killed all of the wolves living there in the 1920s.

This culling led to their primary prey, Elk, exploding in numbers which resulted in overgrazing of willows and aspen. This decimated the beaver population, as their dam material was reliant on what the elk had eaten up. This made marshy areas created by the beavers into streams which actually destroyed many plant species. Bears, magpies, eagles and ravens struggled without the year-round remains of wolf prey to feed on and coyotes became the apex predator.[4] Rodent and fox populations were greatly harmed by the coyotes rule. It wasn't until 1995 that wolves were reintroduced into the park which got the elk population down to a healthy number, amplified the beaver population by 12, halved the coyote population and supported many other plant and animal species.[5] We need wolves in order to have a healthy environment, but following a nihilistic trend, humans remain a critical threat to wolves.

In march of 2021, Wisconsin hunters killed at least 216 wolves in 60 hours.[6] As you've just read the paragraph above, you can guess how this is likely to impact the environment. This hunt also took place during their breeding season. It's likely that many of the wolves killed were either pregnant or new mothers that will not be able to support their pups. The true damage of this hunt is unknown to us, but is deeply apparent to those who lost their lives, mothers, partners or children. Tens of thousands of wolves have been slaughtered by humans in North America, and unfortunately the hunt continues on today. In Idaho, a bill which allows for the killing of 90% of the state's wolves was just signed into law. The motivating force behind the culling is animal agriculture.[7]

Coyotes are members of the dog family that weigh about 20-50 pounds. They live to be 10-12 typically and spend their life with a small pack. Differing from wolves, they often hunt alone or in pairs. This is likely attributed to the smaller nature of their prey. They are most active in the nighttime and spend their days resting in dens. Highly adaptable animals, coyotes are found in deserts, grasslands and forests in the Americas.[8] They have been here for over a million years and even though humans kill around 500,000 of them a year (nearly 1 every minute) their population always seems to bounce back stronger than ever in response.[9] Even though they have this unique ability, it still doesn't warrant trapping them, shooting them from helicopters and hunting them with dogs. Wildlife killing contests often target coyotes in particular, and the manner in which they are beaten to death is brutal.[10] Some of these coyotes who are trapped are then skinned and their fur has been sold to companies such as Canada Goose. Coyotes will be trapped for hours on end with their leg wedged in between steel. Some mother coyotes have even tried chewing off their feet to escape the death trap. Recently, due to years of pressure campaigning, this company has pledged to no longer use new fur in their products.[11] This is a massive win for the coyotes, yet they still face persecution for being alive

Cougars are largely solitary felines (weighing up to 200 pounds) that occupy the Americas, primarily in rocky regions. Cougars are also known as panthers, pumas & mountain lions. Sitting on top of the food chain, they can jump up to 20 feet in the air and hunt anyone in between a moose and an insect.[12] They typically avoid humans, although there have been several documented cougar attacks. This often happens when we get too close to their young or they are starving. We are much more likely to get attacked by a dog than a cougar. However, whenever a cougar attack does occur they are always hunted down and killed. Around 3,000 cougars are killed each year in the U.S[13] and several hundreds are held captive in zoos.

Bears are incredibly powerful, stoic creatures who inhabit forests, arctic tundra's and mountain sides. Eight known species of bears exist, ranging in weight from 60 pounds (Sun Bear) to a whopping 1,000 pounds (Polar Bear).[14] Their minds are vastly intelligent and they are excellent navigators with a strong memory. They are omnivores and eat berries, nuts, seeds, fish and insects mostly. They scavenge quite frequently, and the scent that human campers bring of fresh fruits can captivate them. Improper storage of this food often leads to bear encounters, which are typically nonviolent if handled properly. But if not, it can lead to the bear's execution. Many bears are killed when encountering frightened elk hunters - who are already way too comfortable killing animals. An alternative method that is actually much more effective than a gun at keeping a bear away from you is bear spray. Please, keep it on you if you go out into bear territory so that a possible interaction does not result in the loss of someone's life.

I say this because human interaction is often a death sentence for bears. Around 70% of adult bear deaths are attributed to humans.[15] Many of our encounters with them are due to the fact that their natural habitat continues to get smaller and smaller as humans colonize more and more rural land. If we live in harmony with these animals, then our presence isn't necessarily bad. However, many people who do live out in the country do so for animal farming purposes, and because of that view bears as a threat.

Aside from the human threat bears face in the wild, some bears are used in circuses or are kept captive in zoos. In circuses, bear cubs are often chained by their necks to force them to stand on their hind legs for long periods of time. This behavior is extremely unnatural for them, as they would usually only do this briefly, to gain a greater perspective of their environment. They are trained, through brutal methods, to ride bikes and walk on their front legs in a sort of handstand. Performing is an entirely stressful experience for them and they are kept in small cages when not performing or training. Psychological problems occur in such unnatural and cruel conditions.

Additionally, there are bear farms where these animals are kept in cages often so small they cannot turn around and their bile is collected for "alternative medicine". Stored in their gallbladder, their bile is extracted from them intrusively in ways that often cause infections. In China, around 10,000 bears are kept in these farms and their bile is put in products such as pills and shampoos. [16]

Trophy Hunting

Trophy Hunting is truly one of the most unnecessary and egoic practices I can think of. Hundreds of thousands of animals globally are killed in the wild by hunters, not for their flesh, but almost exclusively for bragging rights. Mounts or whole body taxidermy will immortalize their "accomplishment". In the U.S., trophy animals killed largely consist of bears, cougars, wolves and other native predators. Some U.S hunters feel this is not enough, and will fly to other nations to kill their wild animals. For those who don't want to make the flight, they can still kill exotic, wild animals because in the States we have places specifically dedicated to housing exotic animals for hunters to kill. These are known as "canned hunts", where animals are in enclosed spaces with the hunter and have zero chance of escape. There are several of these facilities in Texas and South Africa. In fact, more rhinoceros, bison and lions exist in this industry than in the their natural habitats.[1] Just like in other areas of animal agriculture, there are breeding facilities to fuel this carnage. 250 of these breeding facilities raise 8,000 lion cubs in South Africa for the purpose of canned hunts. The film Blood Lions depicts this brutal trade.[2]

The methods of killing these animals in captivity and the wild are often cowardly and ineffective. One particularly famous case is of a black-maned lion called Cecil by humans. He lived in Zimbabwe and was lured out with bait, then was shot with an arrow. He then suffered for more than 10 hours as the hunters continued tracking him.[3] Eventually, they found and killed him. Why? For a trophy. Cecil's death rightfully sparked outrage across the globe and placed a social pressure against trophy hunting.

Still, the hunt continues. Americans have been importing an annual average of 126,000 trophies from animals they murdered after spending sometimes hundreds of thousands of dollars to do so. A staggering 1,200 different species are hunted for trophies - the most popular being the "big 5": lions, rhinos, cape buffalos, elephants and leopards.[3]

There is a common argument brought up that the approximately 200 million USD brought into African nations a year via trophy hunting provides an incentive for locals to protect and preserve local wildlife populations. While there is truth to this, it's deeply unfortunate that the incentive to keep them alive is so that foreigners may kill some of them. There are layers to this issue, however, my ground is steady: nobody's life should be for sale, especially when they have literally no say in the matter. The life of this planet deserves respect regardless of if there is an economic incentive to do so. Within the last 50 years, 60% of known wildlife has vanished due both directly and indirectly to human activity.[1] This is why it is of the utmost importance that we protect the wildlife we have left.

Exotic Animal Trade

Wildlife trafficking is estimated to be a 19 billion dollar a year industry.[1] The people who generally participate in this industry do it for money and ego. If their trade wipes out the species, they'll simply move onto the next one. It's far less dangerous for them consequence wise compared to human or drug trafficking and it's much easier to get away with because many law enforcement agencies are not properly informed or trained in this arena. Some areas of the trade are legal, while others are not. U.S. citizens are estimated to presently have 17 million exotic animals in their homes or properties. In comparison, Canadians have about 1.4 million.[2]

Millions of animals are stolen from their homes or bred into existence to be sold off and live an unnatural life in a strange new world. There's no real definition for exotic animals, as the term exotic differs based upon where you live. It's generally used to describe animals such as lizards, monkeys, zebras, tigers, hedgehogs, lions and leopards. Breeding these animals for sale is mostly legal, but the capturing of these animals from the wild to be shipped overseas is criminal in most places. The monetary incentive outshines the loosely upheld laws though, so this trade continues on.

The journey of many of these creatures begins in places like Africa, Australia and the jungles of Brazil. African Gray Parrots have suffered a steep decline in their population, as much as 99% in some regions due to poaching.[3] Otter cubs are being abducted at shockingly high rates. Dogs will be used by poachers to sniff out beaver dens, where they will then violently murder the babies parents, who are fiercely protective of their young. Once captured, they often change hands many times before reaching their final destination. To evade being detected at customs and airport security, drastic measures are taken to hide the stolen animals.[3]

"Parrots might have their beaks and feet taped and be stuffed into plastic tubes that can easily be hidden in luggage, and stolen bird and reptile eggs are concealed in special vests so that couriers can bypass X-ray machines at airports. Baby turtles have been taped so that they are trapped inside their shells and shoved by the dozen into tube socks, and infant pythons have been shipped in CD cases. In one case, a man who was arrested at the Los Angeles airport had Asian leopard cats in a backpack, birds of paradise in additional luggage, and pygmy monkeys in his underwear. Their chances of survival? "We have a mortality of about 80 or 90 percent," says a German customs agent."[4]

Once they arrive, many are sold to zoos, independent owners and pet stores. An investigation conducted by PETA of U.S. Global Exotics led to a raid of their warehouse in Arlington, Texas. Here, approximately 27,000 animals were found in overcrowded conditions without proper access to food or water. Over 400 iguanas had been left in shipping crates without any care for nearly two weeks due to a canceled order. Half of them were found dead. 6,000 of the rescued animals died shortly after being recovered due to their previous neglect and hundreds more were found dead on scene.[4] This was just at one warehouse.

For those who do survive the initial capture, shipment and delivery process, they are often abused and neglected in the hands of their "owner." Many people are simply not equipped to care for these animals, as they are meant to live in the wild. Even in caring hands, it's impossible to provide them with the space and freedom that their natural environments allow for. For example, a free African Gray Parrot spends their typical day flying for miles in gorgeous environments. When in captivity, they often have their feathers clipped to prevent them from escaping. To quote the World Animal Protection Fund: "At least 75% of pet snakes, lizards, tortoises, and turtles die within one year of becoming a pet."[3]

In some instances, those who hold these animals captive make the decision to release them into a wild environment that they are not native to or prepared to survive in. This sometimes causes them to starve to death or to have deadly encounters with humans. In one instance, a man named Terry Thompson, who breeds and imprisons exotic animals, decided to release all of his captive animals before committing suicide. He did so in Ohio, where local authorities have no proper training in how to handle this type of situation using non lethal force (which isn't their strong suit to begin with.) In result, they killed all of the animals released that day: one baboon, two wolves, two grizzlies, three mountain lions, six black bears, 17 lions and 18 Bengal tigers.[3]

When humans intrude upon territories they would not usually venture, aside from to capture and/or kill the native species, they present a threat to themselves and humanity in general. Salmonellosis, for example, is a zoonotic disease carried by many reptiles that can be easily transferred to humans. In fact, "Human contact with reptiles and other exotic animals accounts for 70,000 cases of salmonellosis each year."[5] In the past, we've seen major outbreaks of zoonotic diseases such as Sudden Acute Respiratory Syndrome (SARS), Ebola virus, H1N1, and monkeypox.[6] Presently, we are witnessing COVID-19 unfold across the globe.

While the origins of this illness still remain unconfirmed, the general scientific consensus points to it having nonhuman animal origins. The first major outbreak was linked to a wet market in Wuhan, China where wild animals were sold both alive and dead. The government placed sweeping regulations on the trade following the outbreak.

The Congressional Research Committee states in the report "Wildlife Trade, COVID-19 and Other Zoonotic Diseases" that: "Transmission of zoonotic diseases (i.e., zoonoses) is reportedly facilitated by activities such as land clearing, close human-animal contact (e.g., in live animal markets), hunting and consuming wild animals, and the wildlife trade. SARS-CoV-2 is one of several zoonotic viruses that are likely linked to this trade, which brings humans and wild animals in close proximity. The trade increases the risk of virus transmission between hosts that might not otherwise interact in nature, leading some scientists to contend that wildlife trade can exacerbate the spread of zoonoses."[7]

It's estimated that 75% of today's infectious diseases are a result of zoonosis.[6] Meaning, if we want to prevent major outbreaks that could wipe out millions of humans then we must stop disrespecting & degrading the natural habitats and native species of our planet. If not, then we will continue to experience the consequences of our actions.

Bees

Bees are one of the most ecologically important insects in the world. They're little pollinating superhero's with 5 eyes that can beat their wings up to 200 times per second when in flight![1] There are many species of bees, but today we will be focusing on honeybees. The honeybee hive is occupied by the Queen Bee, whose primary role is reproduction, accompanied by male drones and female workers who have a variety of jobs. The workers and drones can live anywhere between a few weeks to a few months, while the queen can live up to 5 years.[1] Foragers are the bees we most often see, as they are the ones responsible for collecting pollen and nectar. These foragers collect the nectar from around 2 million flowers in order to make 1 pound of honey. On an individual level, a forager bee will make about 1/12th a teaspoon of honey in her entire life.[2] This honey is made to provide the hive with nutrients during the winter seasons, when they'll be in need of it most.

The process of a bee making honey is as follows: "Honey is produced by bees by swallowing nectar, regurgitating it and then repeating this process many times. During this process, their organisms add enzymes to nectar. Bees store honey in honeycombs by regurgitating it into a cell. The cell is then "capped" with wax. This process takes place so that the honey can then be consumed by the bees in the future."[2]

A bee hive is a complex social network that humans are just barely beginning to understand. They communicate using a sort of "dance" based on sight, motion and scent.[3] They can perceive time,[4] lead members of their hive to food, scout for locations for a new hive to be built and alert one another of danger. When the time comes for a new queen to be born, the old queen and half of the hive leave to set up their new home at a location predetermined by scouting bees.[5]

Pesticides, various diseases, habitat loss and climate change has led to a collapse in honey bee and native bee populations. These bees are responsible for pollinating about 130 agricultural crops, making them an absolutely essential species.[6] This, unfortunately, doesn't appear to be enough of a reason for us to respect them and ensure their survival. What humans are after is their honey and labor.

Some honey bees live naturally in the wild or are cared for by a small backyard beekeeper who genuinely wishes them well and protects them from the elements. This is not the case for most honey bees though. Just like other animals raised in industrial agriculture industries, they are put in unnatural conditions, subjected to exploitation and selective breeding practices which are harmful to their species. The white boxes associated with beekeeping exist so that the beekeeper can move the hive from place to place and easily steal their honey. Queen bees are often drugged and their wings are clipped to keep them immobile and passive.

Swarming, when half the hive separates after the birth of a new queen, often causes a decline in honey production since half of the bees leave.[2] This is unacceptable to someone who's sole purpose with these creatures is to take their hard work. This is why they have to keep the queens under their control.

In the winter months, some beekeepers will literally burn entire hives if it's too cold to easily keep them alive.[2] They will also sometimes do this if a disease has emerged in the hive. Due to selective breeding of honeybees, when one hive catches a disease it is highly contagious to other bee colonies because of their genetic similarities. These honeybees, often shipped and moved across country, can easily spread diseases and parasites to the native bee populations.[7]

In addition to honey, some other products that exist in the market because of bee exploitation are: bee pollen, royal jelly (bee milk), beeswax, propolis, bee venom and bee brood.[8] Pollen is collected by bees on little sacs on their legs. Beekeepers sometimes put devices on the front of the hive entrance that will collect some of this pollen from them. This requires them to work much harder for the same amount of pollen to be collected since it's constantly being taken from them. Royal Jelly is a unique fluid fed to the queen and to all larvae under 3 days old. If a new queen needs to be chosen, then that larvae will be continuously fed the royal jelly which will elicit a series of chemical changes in the bees body, leading her to become the Queen. This jelly is stolen from queens-to-be, requiring the nursing bees to work much harder. Beeswax is created on the underside of the bee and is used to build and restore the hive. For however much beeswax that needs to be produced, that bee must consume 8x the amount of honey. The process is very strenuous for the bee and becomes even more so when humans take it from them for cosmetics and candles. Propolis is used as a sort of glue to repair small holes in the hive and as an antiseptic to keep infections from the hive. Bee venom is released when a bee stings someone (or something being used to extract their venom). Their lower abdomen gets ruptured as they try to pull out their stinger, and they experience a dreadful death. Their venom is used medicinally for humans, but at a great cost of their lives. The final product collected from bees is quite disturbing: bee brood. This translates to baby bees. Their bodies are collected and killed at early developmental stages, then eaten by humans.[2]

As you can see, quite literally everything is taken from bees for human benefit. This abuse reaches far beyond just honey bees, but affects every other pollinator on this plant too. How many species of bees do you think there are? 10? 20? 100?..... The answer is 20,000. Of those, about 4,000 are native to North America.[9] So.. where are all these other bees? Well, put simply, the way honeybees are being farmed is pushing other native bee species to the brink of extinction.

A majority of industrial honey beekeepers now migrate their captive bees across the country for profitable pollination. Bees are most extensively used for almond fields, largely in California. In that state, there are so many almond fields that if you were to put them together they would equate to the size of Delaware. This 11 billion dollar industry is quite bee intensive, requiring 10x more bees than Apples (who need the second most bees).[10]

Trucked across the country, these bees are roused from their winter cluster a couple months early in order to pollinate almond fields. Here, they are in a monoculture hellscape. Diverse landscapes are heaven for bees, but modern day massive monoculture fields, doused in toxic pesticides, are deadly for them. About 2.7 million commercial bee hives are recorded in the U.S. In the early weeks of February, approximately 80% of the nation's honeybees are brought to pollinate these 1.4 million acres of almonds.[11] This forced social gathering is a cesspool for deadly diseases to spread. And they do. Just one field may house thousands of hives, not to mention the native bee populations who now have millions of foreign bees to compete with for food. The honeybees often pass on illnesses to already vulnerable bee populations while simultaneously taking away their only food source.

According to EcoWatch: "In the last half decade alone 30 percent of the national bee population has disappeared and nearly a third of all bee colonies in the U.S. have perished."[12]

After 1-2 months of pollinating almonds, the bees are generally moved around the country to pollinate nearly 100 more crops. All the while, the honey they produce and the pollen they collect is robbed from them. Honey bees are natural pollinators; however, they are not meant to travel vast amounts of distances in cramped quarters while having everything they create stolen from them. If we want to support bee colonies, then we have to start at home. One simple step is to not purchase any bee products or support industrialized beekeepers. Instead, support your native pollinators at home! Bees are essential for the pollination of a third of global crops and nearly 90% of wild plant species.[12] Without them, our world would look much different. In order to help local bee (and other pollinator) populations in your community, plant nectar rich, native flowers and plants.[13] Here's a short list of bee-friendly plants (note: make sure to purchase or collect seeds that are pesticide free! Pesticides can kill bees!)

1. Lavender
2. Rosemary
3. Fruit Trees
4. Catnip
5. Oregano
6. Cucumber
7. Squash
8. Melons

Silkworms

Silkworms spin cocoons that protect them while they go through the metamorphosis that allows them to become a moth. The fiber they create and use to spin their cocoons is what humans know as silk. In the silk industry, the process of harvesting this silk typically involves the deaths of those who created them. There is a way of doing this without murder, however it is often not enacted.[1]

Domesticated silkworms, also known as Bombyx Mori, are raised on farms and fed mulberry leaves until they begin spinning their cocoons. Once they've finished spinning themselves a cocoon using the silk secreted from two glands on their head, they begin their transformation. This phase of their life is known as the pupal stage. Unfortunately, their lifecycle will be cut short here and their transformative process is robbed from them. Naturally, when the being is ready to emerge they will eat their way out of their cocoon. This breaks up the silk strands and humans aren't too fond of that. So, a simple solution silk farmers have come up with is to boil them alive while they're in their cocoon. This way, the fibers stay intact and begin unraveling nicely while the creature inside violently dies. Sometimes they instead opt to either freeze or bake them alive. On average, for one pound of silk 3,000 animals are killed.[2]

As mentioned before, there is a way of harvesting silk that doesn't kill the silkworm. There are some companies who utilize the silk after the moth has chewed their way free or others who use a different type of silkworm, known as Samia Ricini, who spin their cocoons with little openings in the end in which they crawl out of.[3] While these methods are far less problematic, the production of silk is still ethically questionable as it does involve the domestication, breeding, farming and exploitation of animals. Ultimately, animals are not ours to use, nor are the things they make.

Humans

Industrial animal agriculture essentially requires human rights violations in order to be profitable. Whether their job is in a slaughterhouse or on a farm, the work is grueling, physically and mentally demanding, emotionally desensitizing and dangerous. Those who have worked in these fields often speak about the horrors of death, disease and misery they've both witnessed and caused. I've heard it firsthand from a couple of men leaving their shift to head back to prison. They told us about how they related to the animals; they were both put behind bars and treated unfairly. We were at first shocked that they were pulling people from prison to do this kind of work, as it is quite the opposite of rehabilitating or healing. Instead of looking into the reason why someone may have committed a certain crime and looking into how to help that person reach a state of mental, emotional and physical security, they send them off to mop blood off the floors of a slaughterhouse. Unfortunately, this is fairly common in the United States.

"There are now twice as many Americans in prison as we have farmers."[1] The book this quote was pulled from was published a decade ago, and since then the disparity has only increased. Daily, the number of small farming operations die off and more people are arrested, often for offenses that they either a) didn't even do or b) shouldn't be a crime anyways. Mandatory minimum sentences have people being locked up for at least two years for the possession of cannabis concentrates in Texas.[2]

Meanwhile, on the other side of a couple imaginary lines, it's next door neighbor Colorado is bankrolling millions in profits. Those incarcerated are then forced to do labor to benefit major corporations, which are increasingly slaughterhouses.

Human death is common in this industry. In 2017, Frank Dwayne Ellington died while on work-release at Koch Foods in Ashland, Alabama. Elsewhere, a worker in Murrayville, Georgia died in 2016 from electrocution. The following year, another person in Nixon, Texas died from excessive chlorine inhalation. In Orange Grove, California someone was crushed to death.[3] The death toll continues on today, and hundreds who are injured but survive lose toes, fingers, arms and hands. This is obviously very dangerous work. Across the nation, poultry and meat packing plants employ at least hundreds of prisoners. It is sometimes their only option for work-release. An investigation by the Southern Poverty Law Center uncovered documents from Georgia and North Carolina showing that since 2015, at least two dozen prison employees had been significantly injured while on duty.[3] Within the same investigation a survey was conducted among poultry plant workers that revealed:

"72 percent of respondents suffered significant work-related injury or illness. Seventeen percent of the workers using sharp tools "suffered a cut serious enough to require some medical attention." Among sanitation workers like Ellington, who have the most exposure to chemicals, 30 percent of respondents said they experienced respiratory problems. The injury rate in the poultry industry is nearly twice the national average for all workplaces. Poultry workers also fall ill at six times the rate of the average American worker."[3]

A vast majority - if not all - of people do not want to work in a slaughterhouse. Line speeds have gone from hundreds of animals slaughtered an hour to thousands. Humans risk being cut by the very knives they use against the animals, kicked in the face by those still alive, slipping on the blood soaked floors or hurt by an animal trying to defend themselves before being murdered. When working on the kill line, there is no time for breaks. A LastWeekTonight episode on YouTube recently featured the abuses occurring to humans in this industry. On that episode they showed a video of a worker urinating beneath the line since there was no time for a bathroom break. This apparently was not the first time this kind of thing had occurred.[4]

Finding people to work in these places is difficult, as the work is less than appealing. As a result, they put slaughterhouses in the lowest income places they can find, which often happen to be in primarily Black and Latino communities. They hire those who have literally no other opportunity for work in their area. In these places often the "good" job is at the slaughterhouse or Walmart. I saw this with my own eyes in Stockton, California. It was one of the most shocking places I've been. Where we were, the streets were littered with human feces, trash and thousands of people with no place to call home. Stray dogs wandered the streets and the animals that humans had claimed as their own weren't in much better conditions. While bearing witness at the slaughterhouse, nine chickens were willingly surrendered to us by workers. They clearly did not want to be there, but they had no other choice. Working there was their only option in a place with one of the highest crime rates and lowest socioeconomic standings in this country.

Statistically, a majority of slaughterhouse workers are People of Color and/or immigrants who are often undocumented.[5] That was clearly displayed in Stockton. Working in a slaughterhouse comes with backlash, such as Post Traumatic Stress Disorder, anger management issues, work-related injuries, high rates of suicide, drug abuse and domestic violence.[6] The job at hand is riddled with known and unknown hazards. Working on the slaughter line is considered one of the most dangerous positions. In a single shift, some working on the poultry slaughter line make up to 20,000 cutting motions.[7] This repetitive motion is mind-numbing and detrimental to their physical health. This makes them prone to injury and disease, which sometimes springs directly out of the bodies they disassemble.

" In early 2008, for example, an unknown neurological illness began afflicting employees at a factory run by Quality Pork Processors in Minnesota, which slaughters 1,900 pigs a day. The diseased workers suffered burning sensations and numbness as well as weakness in the arms and legs. All the victims worked at or near the "head table," using compressed air to dislodge pigs' brains from their skulls. Inhalation of microscopic pieces of pig brain is suspected to have caused the illness. After the CDC investigation, this practice was discontinued."[8]

Due to the unpleasantries guaranteed in this kind of work, it's often hard to find people willing to perform such a terrible, life-threatening job. Aside from situating themselves in low-income communities, one tactic they use, to employee people who won't complain, is by hiring and literally seeking out undocumented immigrants. That way, their workforce will have little knowledge about labor laws, minimum wage, and a constant fear of deportation waved over them if they are to speak up for themselves.[3] Injuries often go unreported unless they render them incapable of working. If so, they will likely be fired and often given no workers compensation.[9] Both plant and animal farms also use these techniques to keep costs low.

Even the slaughterhouses and farms who want to treat humans relatively better than the worst have a difficult time doing so. The reason being is cost. If you're paying your employees a living wage, but your competitor is paying half that much, then the prices for your product are going to be much higher and likely sell less.

You may be thinking: if the work is so terrible, then why not quit? Well, it's not that simple. Most people working in these places would much rather be working literally anywhere else, however their one job opportunity happens to be there.

There are many of us who feel we could never kill an animal, especially hundreds to tens of thousands a day... but many who feel that way are still willing to pay for it. If you're not willing to do something because you feel in your heart it's wrong, then how can you justify paying someone else to do it? If the demand for these products stopped then the factories would have no choice but to stop operating. More ethically aligned companies would hopefully fill the place of the closed CAFOs and slaughterhouses and new work opportunities would be presented to communities who critically need them.

Paralleling the harm of slaughterhouse and farm work, the impact these businesses have on the surrounding communities are virtually always depressing. Massive waste pits filled with urine, blood and feces stink up the nearby towns and often leak into groundwater supplies, rivers and lakes. This can have deadly effects. Nitrates in drinking water, caused largely by pollutants put into the groundwater indirectly or directly by animal farms, have been linked to birth defects, cancer and thyroid dysfunction.[8]

Many farms spray this waste onto fields that are right next to communities, most of which are communities of color. This waste is toxic and makes stepping outside on one of the spray days an undesirable act. Even if you're not by a spray field, being near one of these farms is disgusting. In my town we're a good ten miles from the nearest CAFO, yet on hot summer days when they let the air roll through these farms the smell creeps into town. Sometimes it's so bad that breathing is difficult.

This isn't an isolated incident in the slightest. In fact, " In a study of 226 North Carolina schools, children living within three miles of factory farms had significantly higher asthma rates and more asthma related emergency room visits than children living more than three miles away."[8] For those working in these conditions, their rates of experiencing asthma is 25%. CAFOS emits hydrogen sulfide, which has been linked to neuropsychiatric abnormalities. This may explain why those who live near CAFOs are also more likely to feel stressed, tired, anxious, depressed and angry.[8]

It's not only the people working or living near these facilities that are in danger, but those consuming the flesh coming out of them as well. "In November 1999, the USDA shut down a meatpacking plant for repeatedly failing salmonella tests. The Texas company operating the plant, Supreme Beef Processors, happened to be one of the leading suppliers for the National School Lunch Program. With strong backing from the meatpacking industry, Supreme Beef sued the USDA, eventually won the lawsuit, and succeeded in December 2001 in overturning the USDA's salmonella limits. About 1.4 million Americans are sickened by salmonella every year, and the CDC has linked the nasty, antibiotic-resistant strains of the bug to ground beef. Nevertheless, it is now perfectly legal to sell ground beef that is thoroughly contaminated with salmonella — and sell it with the USDA's seal of approval."[10]

CAFOs are breeding grounds for death and disease. Superbugs, which are antibiotic resistant drugs, are born out of these facilities. These animals are fed numerous amounts of antibiotics throughout their short, miserable lives as a growth hormone and to keep them from dying prematurely. Since subtherapeutic levels are being administered, the bacteria present are given the chance to adapt and survive in these environments. This strengthens them, making them resistant to antibiotics, meaning that if the bacteria were to spread to humans it would have deadly consequences.

Slavery at Sea

On the sea, similar problems arise. In fact, it gets quite worse. If you've ever spent a significant amount of time on the sea, then you know how dangerous it can be. Due to this, tens of thousands of fishermen die every year.[11] Massive ships require a large labor force to operate. These companies have one goal: profit. An easy way to make the most amount of money is to pay your workforce little to no money. This has resulted in slavery at sea.

The same groups responsible for illegal fishing are behind human and drug trafficking as well. In the documentary Seaspiracy, several people formerly enslaved were interviewed. Many of these people were held captive at sea for 6-10 years. They shared their experiences of being hit, having boiling water thrown on them and having an armed guard on board 24/7. They were forced to do difficult, physically demanding work with the threat of death and injury looming over them constantly. Dead human bodies were kept in freezers and some people were thrown overboard.[12]

These fishing vessels aren't only affecting those being forcibly brought onto them, but they greatly affect the local communities as well. On the coast of Africa, The European Union has been clearing the sea of fish. Massive fishing vessels sweep through diverse ecosystems and destroy all they touch. For those who rely on fish for survival in that area, this has been detrimental to their food security and local economy.[12] In the US, 35 billion taxpayer dollars are used to subsidize fisheries.[13] According to the United Nations, this is the same dollar amount we would need to combat world hunger for a year.[14]

World Hunger

" By the turn of the twenty-first century, the world's 800 million hungry people were outnumbered by 1 billion people who were overweight."[8]

Around the world, there are people in nearly every nation that do not have access to clean water or food, while others have an abundance of both. Some of these people slowly starve to death on a street corner, and others in a village next to a dairy farm that used to be a jungle. The problem is not that we have a shortage of food, in many ways we have a surplus. The ways in which we are distributing these essential resources is riddled with inequality. While this is a deeply layered issue that is very much in bed with capitalism, I will largely be speaking of how world hunger directly correlates with animal agriculture.

" In the United States, 157 million tons of cereals, legumes, and vegetable protein are fed to livestock to produce just 28 million tons of animal protein in the form of meat. In contrast, an acre of cereal crops can produce 5x more protein than an acre used for meat production. Tragically, 80 percent of the world's hungry children live in countries with grain surpluses that are fed to animals for consumption by the affluent."[8]

In 2006, the United Nations report, 'Livestock's Long Shadow,' states that: "In simple numeric terms, livestock actually detract more from the total food supply than they provide... In fact, livestock consume 77 million tons of protein contained in feedstuffs that could be potentially used for human nutrition, whereas 58 million tons of protein are contained in food products that livestock supply."[14]

The thousands of CAFOs serving no benefit to society at large could easily be converted into vegan, organic greenhouses. We could grow enough food to feed ourselves, sell to our neighbors and offer to those in need. These facilities would require less land while still employing community members, all without the reliance on animal exploitation. Think about it. If we stop breeding and raising billions of animals for slaughter, feeding them more food than they produce and giving them trillions of gallons of precious water, then we could completely transform our planet in one generation. We can co-create a world where lack is a thing of the past. Our planet creates all we need, all we must do in return is to nurture and respect her and our fellow earthlings.

This change starts with us — our purchasing patterns and random acts of kindness. Invest in (buy from) companies that are in ethical alignment with your values and when possible, grow your own food. Food sovereignty is one of the most empowering things we can do. Nearly all of us can grow microgreens in a jar, start a little backyard garden or an indoor hydroponics system. There is injustice across the board of our industrialized society, so taking back some of the power we've given away can be life changing. The more we rely on others for our basic survival needs, the more we become dependent on those resources. What would we do if they disappeared?

Money Mongering

What's perhaps the most frustrating about all of this, is that government subsidies (also known as taxpayer dollars) are likely the only reason why most factory farms are profitable." Between 1997 and 2005, factory farms saved an estimated $3.9 billion per year because they were able to purchase corn and soybeans at prices below what it costs to grow the crop."[15] This financial booster has allowed them to save 5-15% on production costs. Alternatively, smaller farming operations often receive no subsidies. This has led to more and more small farmers converting to factory farming operations just to stay profitable.

A major funding source for CAFO owners is the Environmental Quality Incentives Program (EQUIP). The original intention of this program was to assist small animal farmers in safely handling waste to better preserve the environment of agricultural land. It has now been distorted into a money pool for CAFO infrastructure, for up to $450,000 per investor over a 5 year period. From 2008-2012, over $7.3 billion in EQUIP funding was approved, with a huge portion being specifically allocated for factory farms.[15]

" The Union of Concerned Scientists has reported that CAFOs received an estimated $100 million per year in EQUIP funding in 2002-2006, with the amount rising to $125 million in 2007."[15]

Hundreds of millions of dollars have been stolen from the public and given to actual environmental terrorists (factory f(h)armers). The industry then charges those who act and rise against them as just that, environmental terrorists. The solution to this problem is quite simple. All the money needed (and more) is already here, we just need to redirect it. If we took the billions of dollars being given to CAFOs and redirected it to repurposing them as veganic greenhouses, then we could transform the course of our species dramatically. Mass amounts of toxic waste would no longer be produced as we stop forcibly impregnating and systematically raising trillions of animals to be slaughtered. Communities once surrounded by disgusting waste lagoons and concentration camps filled with suffering animals would now be blessed with local, organic, year-round produce. Those working would learn a new, life-affirming skill that would be much less dangerous and harmful than their previous job. It's likely that new jobs would be created! The structures are already there, all we need to do is make the change.

Energetic Warfare

We live in a vibrational universe. Every cell in our body, and every other body on this, and likely every, planet is vibrating at a certain frequency. Our vibrational state can be affected by many factors: our emotions, the food we eat, the music/movies we watch, what we say & think, and our general environment.

In regards to our emotions, it's important to understand that in addition to vibrating at a certain frequency, they are also charged with a particular voltage. This voltage causes them to expand or contract based on their state of being.[16] Emotions such as joy, love & excitement vibrate at higher frequencies compared to emotions like fear, anger and despair. When two vibrational beings come into contact, and their energies begin to mingle, resonance often occurs. This means that their vibrations begin to match one another.[17]

So… why am I talking about this? Well, put simply, when one being suffers they produce some of the lowest vibrations possible. Put thousands of individuals together in some of the worst living conditions imaginable and you create a massive density of misery that impacts not just those in it, but the surrounding community as well. Everyone who enters these facilities for work takes that energy home with them, which could be part of the reason why high rates of domestic violence and drug abuse are common among slaughterhouse workers.

I feel that by having tens of thousands of concentrated suffering camps scattered across the world there is a sort of energetic warfare in effect that is detrimental to literally everyone on this planet. This, added with the actual houses of slaughter that exist in nearly every nation, produces a frequency that lowers the collective energy field of the planet. Preventing us from reaching our full potential and living in a state of harmony with one another.

Consciousness, by nature, is expansive. We are ever learning, growing & evolving. This is true of humankind and our fellow earthlings, and likely for beings across the multiverse. Right now, there is mass suppression of consciousness by use of the media, the foods we consume, the products we buy and the trauma we inflict upon others and ourselves. We don't have to live like this. I don't think that life is supposed to be like this. Imagine if every person (both human and non-human) on this planet regularly vibrated at the frequency of joy. How different would this world seem? What could we create together? What would our lives look like?

I dare you to dream; to imagine a peaceful world for all. I dare you to spend time pondering creative solutions to issues you see and then take the risk of implementing them in your life wherever possible. Try. Learn. Grow. Fail. Try again. We don't always get it right the first time, but that's how we learn. I personally have learned a lot from the immense failures of humanity, and I hope that we can all take the knowledge we have gained and not repeat the same mistakes again.

Environmental Benefits of Veganism and Deficits of Carnism

The benefits of veganism and deficits of carnism are deeply interwoven. One major point people often make when it comes to switching to a plant-based diet is cost. There is a common misperception that cutting out meat, dairy and egg products for their alternatives is inherently costly. While this can be true if expensive products are consistently chosen, it can also be false if whole foods are focused on within the diet. Aside from the literal monetary cost for the consumer at checkout, there are a list of other costs that come with our foods that are externalized, which allows companies like McDonalds to have a dollar menu.

"Retail prices of industrial meat, dairy, and egg products emit immense impacts on human health, the environment, and other public assets. These costs, known as "externalities," include water emissions with the potential to heat up the atmosphere, foul fisheries, pollute drinking water, spread disease, contaminated soils, and damage recreational areas. Citizens ultimately foot the bill with billions of dollars in taxpayer subsidies, medical expenses, insurance premiums, declining property values, and mounting cleanup costs."[1]

Animal agriculture is responsible for 20-33% of the world's fresh water consumption, occupies 45% of arable land, is responsible for up to 91% of Brazilian Rainforest destruction, is the leading cause of ocean dead zones, water pollution, habitat destruction and species extinction.[2] According to a report from the United Nations in 2006; " Cattle-rearing generates more global warming greenhouse gases, as measured in CO2 equivalent, than transportation, and smarter production methods, including improved animal diets to reduce enteric fermentation and consequent methane emissions, are urgently needed."[3]

Methane gas is a powerful greenhouse gas that is produced as a byproduct from raising cows. It is considered to be about 80 times more destructive than carbon dioxide exhaust from vehicles over a twenty year timespan in its ability to rapidly warm the planet.[4] With that in mind, know that cows are producing about 150 billion gallons of methane every single day.[2] In the United States, our mass amounts of liquid manure lagoons has boosted us up to the #1 spot in methane emissions from the aforementioned shit pools. In case you're curious about how methane is created, I'd like to enlighten you with this description: " Ruminants, such as cattle, buffalo, sheep, and goats, process their feed through microbial, or "enteric" fermentation in their rumen. This fermentation produces methane that is released by the animals, mainly through their noses and, to a lesser degree, their tailpipes. While this process is what allows ruminants to digest fiber out of grasses that we humans cannot, it adds to livestock's extraordinary climate change toll."[5]

In addition to methane, cows also produce 130x more waste than the entire human population (without any waste treatment programs).[2] This waste often gets into our water streams and acts as a devastating pollutant. To make matters worse, animal agriculture also produces 65%

of the world's human-related nitrous oxide, a gas with a global warming potential 296 times greater than CO2 per pound.[5]

" According to the United Nations Food and Agriculture Organization, the world's livestock contribute to 18% of all annual greenhouse gas emissions. But a recent report from the WorldWatch Institute estimates that livestock could be responsible for as much as 50 percent of all climate changing emissions - making it the most critical influential factor in global warming"[5]

In addition to all of the other pollutants released by animal confinement, about 72-75% of the ammonia emissions reported in the U.S are due to livestock.[6] Confinement only worsens this toxification, as dairy cows kept in CAFOs have been shown to emit 5-10x more ammonia than their counterparts who have the luxury of living directly on this planet. While this and other gasses released by these industries have been found to pose a real threat to this planet and those of us living here. The Environmental Protection Agency only requires companies to report how much they emit... not that they do anything about it. In fact, they have no limit on how much of these harmful gasses they're able to create. One year, a CAFO imprisoning 1,500 cows in Minnesota was so reckless that residents living near them had to be evacuated due to extremely high hydrogen sulfide levels. Hydrogen Sulfide at these extreme levels can cause coughing, vomiting, diarrhea, nausea, headaches and shortness of breath.[5] In areas surrounded by these disgusting factory farms, there is seemingly no escape.

It is unfortunately quite easy for CAFOs to harm the environment with little to no backlash whatsoever. This is partially because the industry is largely self-regulated with essentially no oversight.

" In 2008 the EPA approved an even weaker bill that allows large-scale CAFOs to self certify that they do not intend to discharge pollutants. The public receives no notice of these self-certifications, and there is no required inspection of the CAFO by a regulatory agency. Moreover, a CAFO can have waste spills from many separate sources on the CAFO and recertify each time that its problems have been addressed."[5]

Toxic Shit

Estimates from the US Department of Agriculture state that around 500 million tons of waste are produced by factory farming every year.[7] This figure is 3x higher than the waste generated by this nation's human population, and there is virtually no proper waste treatment occurring. This means that a majority of it is sprayed onto fields, held in massive manure pits and often leaks into groundwater, rivers, streams, lakes, ponds and the ocean. Animal agriculture is the leading cause of ocean dead zones for this reason, combined with their excessive use of fertilizers and other harmful chemicals on the crops fed to animals. According to a report conducted by the U.S. Environmental Protection Agency, waste from pig, chicken and cow "production" has polluted 35,000 miles of rivers in 22 states while also having significantly contaminated groundwater in at least 17 states.[5]

Environmentally, the enormous quantities of pigs raised in relatively small areas is devastating to the local ecology. The main problem arises in their shit. Pigs produce 3x more fecal matter than humans do, all without a proper waste management system. Pig CAFOs house a minimum of 1,000 animals, with the largest in Iowa confining 24,000.[8] In these metal sheds, they all shit onto the floor of their cell, which then falls through the slats, gathers up and generally is pumped into either a septic tank underground or a lagoon, many of which are open-pit. Heavy metals, ammonia, cyanide, hydrogen sulfide, phosphates and nitrates are all found in these lagoons of toxic sludge.

" The lagoons themselves are so vicious and venomous that it is often impossible to save the people who fall into them. A few years ago, a truck driver in Oklahoma was transferring pig shit into a Smithfield lagoon when he and his truck went over the side. It took almost three weeks to recover his body. In 1992, when a worker making repairs in a lagoon in Minnesota began to choke to death on the fumes, a worker dived in after him, and they died the same death. On another occasion, a worker who was repairing a lagoon in Michigan was overcome by the fumes and fell in. His fifteen year old nephew dived in to save him but was overcome; the workers older brother dived in to save them but was overcome; then the workers father dived in. They all died in pig shit."[9]

One of the most common ways CAFOs dispose of their waste is by spraying them on fields. In areas near these massive spray fields, the people living there literally can't go outside comfortably if they're spraying. Some people have stepped outside and been so overwhelmed by the putrid stench that they collapse.[10] Within the house, attempts to keep the odors out are helpless. Keeping all doors and windows shut keeps the worst of the odors out, but there are times where the food they consume is laced with the taste of pig shit.[9] These companies are not only heartlessly tormenting the animals they enslave, but they are also destroying the communities they have invaded.

"Smithfield Foods, the largest and most profitable pork processor in the world, killed 27 million hogs in 2007. That's a number worth considering. A slaughter-weight hog is 50 percent heavier than a person. The logistical challenge of processing that many pigs each year is roughly equivalent to butchering and boxing the entire human populations of New York, Los Angeles, Chicago, Houston, Philadelphia, Phoenix, San Antonio, San Diego, Dallas, San Jose, Detroit, Indianapolis, Jacksonville, San Francisco, Columbus, Austin, Memphis, Baltimore, Fort Worth, Charlotte, El Paso, Milwaukee, Seattle, Boston, Denver, Louisville, Washington DC, Nashville, Las Vegas, Portland, Oklahoma City, and Tuscan."[9]

Smithfield isn't the only company causing this type of destruction, they're just one of them. A competitor of theirs caused the biggest environmental spill in U.S history in 1995. A 120,000 square foot lagoon ruptured and released 25.8 million gallons of waste into the headwaters of the New River in North Carolina. The toxic goo was so harmful that people reported being burned to the touch. It took about two months to make its way to the ocean, and by that time over a million fish died.[9] In addition to being susceptible to ruptures, open air lagoons are vulnerable to being overwhelmed by a light rain, and when hurricanes occur all hell breaks loose.

As you can see, what we feed or inject into animals eventually makes its way into some form of water somewhere. With access to clean water depleting globally, it is more important now than ever to closely monitor what we allow in our waterways. Humans are not the only ones affected by these pollutants, we just happen to be the main species causing them.

Fish are perhaps the most plentiful victim of water toxification. One way this contamination occurs is through steroids. Cows are sometimes given steroids via ear implants which slowly release the anabolic steroid trenbolone. Ten percent of these steroids pass right through the cows, according to a German study. It's then released through their waste, which often ends up in nearby waterways. This can negatively affect the wildlife living there. For example, male fathead minnows who lived downstream from a farm utilizing these drugs displayed low testosterone levels and small heads. The water they were living in contained 4x more steroids than water upstream from the farm.[5]

Now, let's look at a nasty microbe. Pfiesteria piscicida is a multi form microbe responsible for violently killing hundreds of millions of fish and harming at least dozens of humans. It can arise from algae blooms following the havoc of a shit spill. Hoards of fish appear to eat the algae and this allows a deadly form of pfiesteria to arise. This microbe eats the blood cells, tissues and skins of fish - making it so that they seemingly dissolve. It can also scavenge human blood cells, attacking the bodies of fishermen. Intense memory loss (not being able to find their way home), headaches, blurry vision and respiratory problems can occur. Some of those studying it in laboratories then got exposed, forgot their names and had trouble completing basic tasks. Recovery can take years.[9]

Water Crises

A staggering 322 *billion* gallons of water is used *every day* in the United States alone![11] 80-90% of this water is directly funneled into our agricultural practices, with feed crops for animal ag consuming 56% of total water usage.[2] In the world, we have reached the tipping point of a global water crisis. In the midst of this epidemic which has already led to regional conflicts, disputes, disease and worsened living conditions, we are still actively and ignorantly contributing to the leading cause of water consumption and pollution. In order to produce one 1/3 pound hamburger, at least 660 gallons of water must be used.[12] This means that eating one hamburger is the equivalent of the average American showering for two entire months. Our dietary choices have the most significant impact on our personal water use.

I've already spoken in depth about how animal agriculture impacts our world's oceans. But because of how important this particular issue is, I would like to emphasize it one last time. Presently, our oceans are dying. If our oceans die, we are likely to die. It's that simple. A majority of the air we breathe doesn't come from the rainforests (although they are important), but actually the ocean.[13] If we continue stealing all reachable life from our oceans then we will likely eliminate ourselves in the process. The world's fish population is collapsing. According to the United Nations Food and Agriculture Organization, roughly three quarters of all the fisheries are either fully exploited, overexploited or depleted.[14] The world fish population has depleted drastically over the past several decades, with humans being 100% responsible. Compared to the 56 + billion farmed animals killed a year, roughly 2.7 *trillion* sea creatures are caught and killed annually. Approximately a third of these caught are then ground up and put in feed for farmed pigs, cows and even fish.[5] Recent estimates state that we will have *no reachable fish* in our oceans by 2048. If current production rates continue, then that date may come much sooner than anticipated.

In addition to simply not eating fish, one way we can help stop this from happening is by demanding that our lawmakers petition to stop government subsidization of the fishing industries.

"In an exhaustive survey of 152 countries, scientists at the University of British Columbia found that ocean-faring nations spent $22 billion on harmful subsidies in 2018, or 63 percent of the total amount expended to support the global fishing industry."[15]

Without our support, this industry will collapse.

Land Abuse & Soil Erosion

Globally, livestock production is the largest user of land on the planet, and in my educated opinion, it's a waste of perfectly good earth. In the U.S, 260 million acres of public land largely managed by the Bureau of Land Management and the US Forest Services is leased to farmers for grazing cows.[16] Often, wild animals fall victim to this arrangement, especially predators who are seen as a threat.

" 33 % of the planet's arable land is dedicated to growing feed crops, which are energy-intensive to raise."[5]

Half of all fertilizer in the US & Canada is used on these feed crops. In the UK, that percentage spikes to nearly 70%.[5] This fertilizer can be detrimental to the health of the soil microbiome, in turn affecting the health and viability of the plants growing from it. Healthy soil is essential for healthy crops. Plants grown in nutrient-deficient soil will echo the well-being of their environment in themselves as well. The fruits and veggies we eat nowadays have less nutrients in them than they did 50-100 years ago because of our unsustainable farming practices. This is actively affecting everyone reading this, even if until now you were oblivious to it. Healthy plants need healthy topsoil; unfortunately, the world's topsoil is eroding away at unprecedented rates.

"According to the United Nations Food and Agriculture Organization, the world is losing an equivalent of 10 to 15 million acres of farmland through erosion each year... Every year, the United States loses nearly 2 billion tons of soil, making farmlands less fertile and setting off a cascade of destructive consequences."[5]

Strong soil is generally created by a healthy, diverse ecosystem that allows for plants to root deep into the ground and natural systems to operate as intended. The common form of agriculture nowadays, monoculture, is harmful for soil health. Using large machines to break up the soil in a process known as tilling can actually be quite destructive, especially when this process is repeated yearly. This is now becoming common knowledge among those in the farming community, so more and more farmers are joining the no-till movement.[17] However, tilling the soil is only a part of the problem.

Large, hooved animals overgrazing in a focused area weakens the soil and allows for the wind to blow it away, often landing in streams and other waterways. Rotational grazing systems can reduce this drastically, but since that practice certainly isn't common, our topsoil is withering away. Concentrated methods of raising animals coupled with massive mono crop fields relying heavily on pesticides creates a disastrous situation. This irresponsible system of feeding and raising the animals classified as livestock is responsible for 85% of soil erosion in the US.[18]

Approximately 95% of the world's food is reliant on healthy topsoil. It is essential for our survival. Within the last 150 years about half of the most productive soil has disappeared and cropland soil in the US is eroding 10x faster than we can replenish it. It's estimated by experts in the United Nations that within the next 60 years we will run out of topsoil if we continue at this pace.[19] I highly recommend watching the documentary Kiss the Ground to learn more.

Deforestation

Deforestation is another significant cause of soil erosion. The destruction of old growth forests is perhaps the worst, because of how extensive their root systems are and how much life they nurture. There are many reasons for deforestation, sometimes it's for lumber or paper products. Most often, however, it's to clear land for agricultural purposes.

Globally, we are losing our rainforests at a rate of an acre per second.

Gone.

An acre of rainforest was just demolished.[20]

The driving force behind rainforest destruction is animal agriculture. Entire forests are being cut down to graze animals and grow genetically modified soybeans and other crops to ground into feed for the animals being exploited. Over 80% of the rainforest in Brazil was destroyed for cattle ranching when you take into account soybean production for the cows being used.[21] Animal feed constitutes 80% of the world's soybeans.[22] This percentage is only growing by the second. It's estimated that every day, over 100 plant, animal and insect species are lost due to rainforest destruction. At this rate, it's likely that all tropical rainforests will be cleared within the next 40 years.[20] This onslaught isn't happening without a fight, it's just unfortunate that one side is comfortable with murder. After the Forest Code passed in Brazil, many people that spoke out in protection of the rainforests were killed. For example, Dorothy Stang, a nun who lived in Para, Brazil was murdered for speaking out against the industry.[10]

According to the World Animal Foundation, "Already 56 million acres of land are used to feed farmed animals, while only 4 million acres produce plants for human consumption. It takes 20 times less land to feed someone on a plant based diet than it does to feed meat eaters."[23] If everyone in the world who could, did adopt a plant-based diet, then we could simply convert part of the land presently used for animal agriculture. We could sustain our population while rehabilitating and reforesting the land that we no longer need to use. This also means we wouldn't have to cut down any more of the rainforest. All the land we need we already have available, it's just being used terribly.

Hope for a Healthy Planet

Now, while all of that is quite daunting, I would like to emphasize that it is not too late to redirect our momentum. There is hope. Presently, about 40% of the usable land is occupied by and for animal agriculture. I recently began working with an organization called United In Heart with a goal to transition a majority of the world to a vegan lifestyle and to reclaim the land previously used for animal agriculture for the planet. Their goal is to take 41% of the land previously used for animal ag and to simply reforest it. Quoting from their website, " A 2019 publication in Science indicates that if we add one trillion trees to the Earth, we will cut the atmospheric carbon pool by 25% and return to the safe zone with respect to global warming."[24]

By simply stopping the mass murder of every other species on this planet, no longer pillaging our seas and polluting them with fishing nets, relying on plant based foods grown locally and planting a ton of trees; we could completely change the planetary path in THIS generation. We **can** do it and it doesn't even have to be that hard. But it starts with us.

When choosing to not eat animals you automatically retract your support of the animal agriculture industry and begin purchasing products that are much less destructive (maybe even helpful). A study conducted by the University of Oxford even found that cutting meat and dairy products from one's diet led to a 73% reduced carbon footprint. The same researchers found that if this switch was made globally then then our collective use of farmland could reduce by 75%. To put this into perspective, that is the total mass of the United States, China, Australia and the European Union combined.[25] That's massive! We could revive lost habitats and species, clean our air and waterways and save ourselves by simply eating a plant based diet and reforesting our world.

Health Benefits of Veganism and Deficits of Carnism

Now, I would like to say before starting this segment that just because a food is labeled vegan does not necessarily mean it is healthy. Eliminating animal products from your diet is likely to be followed by health benefits, but you can live off of vegan junk food and still be having a difficult time health wise because whole plants are what's really healing for the body. Abstaining from the consumption of animal products will almost certainly have a positive impact on your physiology, but in order to reap the full benefits of a plant-based diet, nutrition must really be considered.

The benefits I am about to discuss largely come from eating a holistic vegan diet - not from eating processed meat alternatives, potatoes and vegan chocolate every day. If you want to eat those things then go for it! Those items are delicious in moderation, but if we want to see results in our physiology then we must eat nourishing foods. This may mean different things to different people. For me, if I eat too much processed sugar and gluten my body breaks out in a rash which acts as an alarm system. Use these types of things as cues to see if you're eating the right foods for you, and maybe consider getting a food sensitivity test to see what works best for your body. We all have different vessels with different needs.

Now, as I mentioned earlier, when I went vegan I was able to whack diabetes out of the ballpark and lower my bad cholesterol levels significantly, as well as, basically make my hypoglycemia disappear. These are all common side effects of eating life affirming foods. Many documentaries such as What The Health & The Game Changers discuss a lot of anecdotal evidence of stories similar to my own. Some of which are much more significant and really impactful. While anecdotes are powerful, you can find one to support just about anything. So let's take a look at the overwhelming scientific consensus for a moment.

In general, those who follow plant based diets have higher intakes of fiber, antioxidants, magnesium, folate, potassium, and vitamins A, C & E. Vegans also tend to have lower BMI and weigh less overall.[1] This obviously varies case by case, and in some instances a vegan diet may help someone gain weight or lose it. I've known people who have struggled to lose weight be able to drop quite a few pounds when adopting a plant based diet, and others who were dealing with an eating disorder be able to regain control of their health and mental well-being while gaining a healthy amount of weight with the assistance of this lifestyle switch.

Diabetes

The adoption of a plant-based diet has been shown to have a remarkable effect on those with or in the process of developing diabetes. Globally, around 422 million people have diabetes and in 2019 diabetes was determined to be the direct cause of 1.5 million deaths.[2] Here in the U.S, one out of every ten people has diabetes. This equates to about 34 million people, while 88 million adults are prediabetic and are likely to develop the disease if they don't make substantial lifestyle changes.[3] Quite serious ailments can emerge as a result of developing diabetes, such as blindness, cardiovascular disease, kidney disease, limb amputation and death.[2] This is why taking preventative measures is so important.

Diabetes is divided into two main categories — type 1 and type 2 — which both revolve around the body's ability to regulate blood sugar, also known as glucose. Our bodies cells are fed by glucose, but in order to enter the cells it needs a sort of key, known as Insulin. When our body's blood sugar rises, it sends a signal to our pancreas to release insulin so that our cells can then use that sugar as energy. Typically, those with type 1 diabetes do not produce enough (or any) insulin and those with type 2 don't respond to insulin properly and/or don't make enough of it.[4] Due to this, their blood sugar levels rise uncontrollably which can cause moderate to severe damage to the body.

Type 1 diabetes is generally considered to be an autoimmune response and is diagnosed in the early years of someone's life. Recently, several studies have shown a significant link between consuming cows milk as a child and the development of type 1 diabetes and other autoimmune diseases.[5] Of those that have diabetes, about 90-95% of them have Type 2. It's usually seen in adults who are overweight, live a sedentary lifestyle and consume high volumes of animal products. It is both reversible and preventable with regular exercise and a healthy plant-based diet.[4]

In 2019, the Harvard T.H. Chan School of Public Health published a study displaying that the risks of developing type 2 diabetes can be cut by 23% by simply eating a plant-based diet. Those who consumed a whole foods plant-based diet were even better off.[6] Food truly is medicine. This goes even further in a study published in 2018 in the BMJ Open Diabetics Research & Care journal. Here they found that "plant-based diets were associated with significant improvement in emotional well-being, physical well-being, depression … general health, HbA1c levels, weight, total cholesterol, and low-density lipoprotein cholesterol, compared with several diabetic associations' official guidelines."[7] And the real miracle here is that a whole foods plant based diet has even been found to reverse type 2 diabetes in some individuals by resolving insulin resistance, the root cause of diabetes.

While there is presently no known cure for type 1 diabetes, research shows that a whole foods plant based diet can help manage the symptoms significantly and possibly prevent it from occurring in the first place. According to Cyrus Khambatta, PHD, a whole foods plant based diet can lead to more predictable blood glucose levels, boost insulin sensitivity while reducing insulin use by more than 40% within 6 months and increase blood flow therefore decreasing the risk of nerve & kidney damage.[7]

Heart Disease

According to the Center for Disease Control, "One person dies every 36 seconds in the United States from cardiovascular disease."[8]

Cardiovascular disease, also known as heart disease, is a blanket term used to describe many conditions that are often derived from atherosclerosis, which is: "a condition that develops when a substance called plaque builds up in the walls of the arteries. This buildup narrows the arteries, making it harder for blood to flow through. If a blood clot forms, it can block the blood flow. This can cause a heart attack or stroke."[9] For nearly 100 years, heart disease has been the leading cause of human death.[10] So, what causes it? Saturated fat is the main known culprit when it comes to plaque build up. Can you guess what the primary source of saturated fat is in most people's diets? You probably can.

Yes, it is animal products. Plaque is a conglomerate of fats, proteins and immune system cells that together form a greasy layer of ick that sticks to the walls of our arteries. When we consume foods like meat, butter, milk, cheese and ice cream we are loading our bodies with dietary cholesterol, animal protein and saturated fat. Several studies have highlighted how animal products dramatically increase the amount of plaque that builds up along our arteries, while a plant based diet can reverse this process. This research has been so effective that dozens of insurance companies have covered a year-long lifestyle intervention program, by Dr. Dean Ornish, as an alternative to surgery for heart disease patients.[10]

While it is the leading cause of death globally and accounts for 1 in every 4 deaths in the U.S,[8] this disease clearly isn't as inescapable as many have been led to believe. A review published in the Progress in Cardiovascular Diseases recently revealed that a plant-based diet can reduce the risk of death from cardiovascular disease by 40% while reducing the risk of coronary heart disease by the same percentage. Additionally, they found that 91% of their patients showed great improvement in blood flow through their arteries as a result of the diet. Weight loss and lower blood pressures were also observed. In some cases, heart disease has even been reversed by a plant based diet.[11] This is something modern day medicine has never done, but a simple diet switch can.

Cancer

The World Health Organization (WHO) has classified bacon and sausage as carcinogenic.[12] The word carcinogen means a "cancer-containing substance." WHO also classifies processed meat as a group one carcinogen, in the same group as cigarettes, asbestos and plutonium. Red meat has been classified as a group two carcinogen.[13] In the US, 1 in every 4 deaths is from cancer.[14] This isn't even surprising when you take into account how much meat is consumed by the average American (274 pounds of meat per year, not including sea life).[15] On the other hand, when you take a look at cultural regions who consume much less meat and dairy products compared to the western world you'll typically see much lower incidents of cancer and cardiovascular disease.[10]

There have been several scientific and observational studies done that note the protective effect a plant based diet has against cancer cells building. Doctors aware of this effect who have patients' health in mind often use a plant based diet as a preventative method against cancer alongside medical treatments. Many of us wait until something goes wrong to take action. While in some ways that makes sense, when it comes to disease prevention it is extremely harmful. An analysis of autopsies of women in their 40s found that 39% of them had breast cancer that was too small to be detected by mammograms. These scans can only begin to detect tumors once they've reached the size of about 2 billion cells.[12] Many are caught much later in their development.

Furthermore, "Research funded by the National Cancer Institute, the National Institutes of Health, and the World Cancer Research Fund, found that women who consumed 1/4 to 1/3 cup of cow's milk per day had a 30% increased chance for breast cancer. One cup per day increased the risk by 50%, and 2-3 cups were associated with an 80% increased chance of breast cancer."[16] A huge reason behind this is that the higher our estrogen levels are, the more likely we are to develop breast cancer. Dairy products are full of mammalian estrogen which can lead to a person's menstrual cycle starting earlier, lasting longer and being more uncomfortable in general. The longer our reproductive life cycle, the higher the chances we have of developing breast cancer. Doctors know this, which is why anti estrogen drugs such as Tamoxifen are used as preventative measures against cancer.[10] What if, instead, we addressed why people's estrogen levels are so high in the first place and take proper corrective actions? Nearly 40,500 people die of breast cancer annually,[12] which is deeply unfortunate, especially because it is preventable.

Now, let's talk about Insulin-like Growth Factor 1 (IGF-1). Cell growth is fed by IGF-1. The more IGF-1 present in the bloodstream, the more fuel tumors have to multiply. Animal based proteins are the main source of IGF-1, thus increasing the risk of cancer dramatically. One study published showed that just two weeks of a plant based diet and regularly walking led to a 20-30% increase in the body's ability to eliminate cancer causing cells. There are a multitude of studies linking animal product consumption to a higher risk of cancer and death while a vegan lifestyle has been linked to reduced rates of the same ailments, as well as all of the 15 leading causes of death globally.[12]

One specific study was essential in our understanding of the role of diet in regards to disease. A mold toxin believed to be the most carcinogenic substance in the world called Aflatoxin was involved in a critical (and unethical) study showing how nutrition is directly related to our ability to activate or deactivate cancerous cells. For a long time, European & American scientists believed that higher protein (specifically animal protein) intake led to a healthier population. What the following study shows is the exact opposite.

To quote Thomas Campbell in The China Study, " Indian researchers had studied two groups of rats. In one group, they administered the cancer-causing Aflatoxin, then fed a diet that was composed of 20% protein, a level near what many of us consume in the West. In the other group, they administered the same amount of aflatoxin, but then fed a diet that was only composed of 5% protein. Incredibly, every single animal that consumed the 20% protein diet had evidence of liver cancer, and every single animal that consumed a 5% protein diet avoided liver cancer. It was a 100 to 0 score, leaving no doubt that nutrition trumped chemical carcinogens, even very potent carcinogens, in controlling cancer."[10]

Doctor Campbell found in his 27 year study that animal protein, specifically casein (found in cow's milk) activates cancer growth while plant protein does the opposite. This finding is significant when you factor in the statistic from the American Cancer Society that men in the US have a 47% chance of developing cancer in their lifetime while women have a 38% chance. As the research in The China Study clearly displays, cancer is not inevitable. It is controllable, preventable, and reversible.[10] To learn more, I highly recommend reading the book 'The China Study.'

Sick Care System

So, with all we've learned, why are plant based diets not being used everywhere to treat and prevent illness? Established medical institutions *especially in the United States* are in the business of treating sick people, **not curing** them. This is not necessarily the intention of many doctors, however, most hospitals (and doctors) quite literally profit on a continually ill population. This can be seen in the documentary What The Health, when the director goes to speak to a heart surgeon who uses a plant based diet to help treat his patients. Before they even reach the front door, the hospitals' public relations person stops them and blatantly states that the hospital makes money off of these surgeries and cannot risk an interview that would decrease their profit revenues. This is extremely disheartening, but really brings the health situation of our nation and planet into perspective.

Foods to Consume For Healthy Vegan Living

Now that we've addressed the ethics, environmental and health aspects of veganism, it's time to learn how to transition into a vegan lifestyle! One of the biggest factors in this is food. Many people nowadays are misinformed or just simply unaware of how to eat a balanced, nutrient-rich diet. I mean, I know there were days in my childhood where I thought I was doing well eating steak, cheese-its and some juice. My diet has improved vastly since then.

Here we're going to discuss what foods to eat, but this will obviously shift if you have any allergies or food intolerances. What I would like to encourage, as long as it's not harmful for you, is to try everything vegan you can! I used to be such a picky eater and I still definitely have my preferences, but when I first made the switch I decided that I had to try new things and it worked out tremendously for me. I mean, I literally just learned that I love mangos a couple of months ago! So, I urge you to try new things! Expand your taste buds and get cookin if you can. Now, for nutritional aspects.

Here is a vegan food pyramid that I created and mostly follow. There are several online that differ and I'm not yet a nutritionist so don't take this as scripture. But it is a good place to start. A good rule of thumb is to simply eat the rainbow.

Vegan food pyramid

Oils & sweets

legumes, nuts, seeds & plant milks

SEEDS

Whole grains

Veggies

fruits

Fruits & veggies are an excellent base for a vegan diet. Leafy greens are a substantial source of calcium, Vitamin A, C & K, Magnesium, Potassium & Fiber![1] My favorites are kale, spinach and lettuce but there are plenty of others to try such as collards, cabbages and turnip greens. An easy way to get your greens is to eat salads! When I was younger I thought salads were kinda boring, but now I like loading them up with lettuce, kale, spinach, cucumber, walnuts, tomatoes, sprouts, sometimes crispy mushrooms or tofu and my favorite dressing which just so happens to be called Goddess Dressing. You could also add in some beans, rice & avocado and make yourself a taco salad or switch it up about a thousand different ways. If you think you don't like salad, I can almost promise you that there is at least one salad out there that you'll fall in love with.

Some other great veggies include broccoli, peas, carrots, sweet potatoes, onions, bell peppers and cauliflower - to name a few. In just one cup of chopped broccoli you'll find your daily needed intake of Vitamin K and twice your needed serving of Vitamin C. Peas are packed with 9 grams of both fiber and protein in one cup along with vitamins A, C & K with some B vitamins as well. Sweet Potatoes are packed with Fiber and rich in nutrients such as Potassium, and Beta Carotene, as well as, Vitamins A, B & C. One cup of chopped carrots contains 4x your recommended daily value of Vitamin A, which supports eye health immensely. Tomatoes (which are fruits technically) contain powerful antioxidants such as Lycopene, Beta Carotene, Lutein and zeaxanthin.[2]

As you can see, veggies contain a vast nutritional profile that differs depending on that vegetable we're talking about. Cauliflower boiled and blended makes an excellent base for any noodle dish, as well as the base of a soup. Veggies can be eaten raw or cooked or in soup form or even fried. There's tons of ways to enjoy them. You can throw a fun mix together with some rice or noodles as a stir fry, stick them in tacos or burritos or a salad! They're incredibly versatile. A healthy plant based diet is reliant on veggie intake, so have some fun with them! There are literally thousands of cookbooks (other than this one) and recipes online that will teach you how to make delicious meals. Do some shopping around!

Fruits are another important cornerstone for a plant based diet. I personally eat a large bowl of mixed fruit for breakfast almost every morning that differs day to day. Most often it includes apples, oranges and berries with some granola and vegan yogurt. I also really enjoy some chocolate in there as well. Sometimes I throw in pineapple, watermelon, mango or whatever fun fruit is calling my name that day. Some people, like my partner, find that eating fruit later in the day after having eaten veggies is upsetting to the stomach. This definitely isn't a universal truth and may not apply to you, but it may be something to think about if fruit doesn't settle well in your belly sometimes. I generally eat a majority of my fruit in the morning time and I find it very energizing.

An example of nutritionally plentiful fruits are: apples, blueberries, oranges, dragon fruits, bananas, avocado, strawberries, pineapple, durian, cherries, olives, watermelon, grapefruit, peaches and kiwis. Fiber is abundantly present in apples, oranges, dragon fruit, mangos, avocado, durian and cherries. Oranges contain 91% of your daily needed Vitamin C along with potassium, folate and vitamin B1.. Virtually all of these fruits have plentiful amounts of antioxidants and anti-inflammatory properties, blueberries especially.[3] Tons of vitamins and minerals are found in these fruits, so I highly recommend eating fruit every day if possible.

Our next section is whole grains. These include Oats, whole-grain corn, popcorn, brown rice, whole rye, wild rice, whole-grain barley, buckwheat, bulgur, triticale, millet, quinoa, sorghum and 100% whole wheat flour. Protein, fiber, B vitamins, antioxidants and trace minerals are prominent in these whole grains. When regularly consumed, these grains have been linked with reduced rates of cardiovascular disease, obesity, type 2 diabetes and some forms of cancer. Additionally, by promoting healthy bowel movements, whole grains help keep our colons thriving. Americans are in desperate need of more foods in this category, because according to a WebMD article written by Kathleen Zelman, "the average American eats less than one serving per day, and over 40% never eat whole grains at all."[4]

Easy ways to incorporate whole grains into your diet could be eating a bowl of oatmeal, whole grain cereal or whole grain toast for breakfast. Choosing brown or wild rice instead of white with a nice veggie stir fry is an easy switch! When purchasing pasta, choose whole grain pasta - either brown rice or whole wheat. When baking, consider choosing the whole grain options and get the benefits from eating some sweet baked goods. A nice snack of popcorn with some salt, nutritional yeast and a drizzle of coconut oil is another delicious option.

Following our base of fruits, veggies & whole grains is legumes, nuts, seeds and dairy alternatives. Legumes encompass beans, lentils and peas. There are about a dozen or so legumes so you're destined to find at least a few that you enjoy. My favorites are chickpeas and black beans. They're great to cook & eat with rice, in salads, tacos, burritos and soups. Most legumes are fairly low in fat and calories while being high in protein, fiber, B Vitamins, iron, folate, calcium, potassium, phosphorus and zinc. Beans share a similar nutritional profile to meat, but with no saturated fat, cholesterol or death.[5] They also happen to be fairly low in cost.

Diets consisting primarily of rice, beans and leafy greens happen to be the cheapest diets in most places. This is fantastic because of how nutritionally dense legumes are. In just 1 cup of black beans 15 grams of fiber can be found, which is about half the recommended daily value. Antioxidants are packed into these powerful foods which help reduce our bodies oxidative stress levels, helping prevent and heal dis-ease within the body.[5] If at all possible, make sure to include legumes into your diet regularly, eating a serving a day several times a week.

Building upon this nutritionally dense foundation, we now will take a look at nuts & seeds. Quoting this Harvard paper titled Why Nutritionists Are Crazy About Nuts, "Mounting evidence suggests that eating nuts and seeds daily can lower your risk of diabetes and heart disease and may even lengthen your life."[6] The value of nuts differs, but most contain a solid amount of fat, protein, fiber, vitamins and minerals. Brazil nuts are special for their high concentration of Selenium, with just one nut containing 100% of the suggested daily value.[7] Being packed with antioxidants, nuts can neutralize the free radicals in our bodies which cause cellular damage and promote disease.

Consuming food that works for us instead of against us... what a concept!

Seeds are tiny yet mighty. They are filled with iron, calcium, magnesium and phosphorus while acting as a reliable source of healthy fats, minerals and fiber. Chia seeds and flaxseeds are both great sources of nutrition while being incredibly multi-purpose. They're both great to pack into smoothies and used as an egg substitute when combined with water and some time. Sunflower seeds make an excellent snack and offer the body antioxidants such as vitamin E. Pumpkin seeds can serve a similar purpose while being rich in Zinc.[8]

On a less whole-foods note, we have dairy substitute products. Some of these are quite easy to make at home, such as virtually every plant milk. However, the benefit of buying them in store is that they come fortified with tons of vitamins and minerals. These are foods that should be consumed in moderation, while serving their purpose. When I first went vegan, I was a little addicted to Silk Chocolate soy milk, which conveniently contained all of my needed B12 and 8 grams of protein in 8oz. These plant milks are great for cereals, smoothies, baking and drinking.

Other products such as vegan yogurt are quite delicious in my opinion. I like to enjoy it with granola and tons of fruit. Plant based cheeses are usually more so for taste than nutritional value, which is why I suggest occasional consumption only.

I would also consider meat alternatives to be in this section as well. While products like Beyond Meat are nutritionally dense and delicious, they are fairly processed and high in fat. If you're going for a health-focused approach, then I would caution moderation here. If you're just vibin with veganism for the animals, then have as much as you want! I personally have meat alternative products 1-3 times a week on average, which I'm working to reduce further.

At the top of our pyramid we've got oils and sweets. Seasonings could also be placed here as well. Oils are essentially just fat so it's good to be aware of how much oil you're cooking with on a regular basis. There are tons of vegan goodies out there that could easily be classified as junk food. When you're really craving a chocolate bar or cake or whatever sweet then go for it. But with any diet, eating sugary processed foods isn't particularly healthful in the long run. Just use your thinker and you'll be alright.

Before moving on, I'd like to debunk some nutrition myths, starting with one Vitamin that is discussed a lot when speaking about a plant based diet. What I'm referring to is Vitamin B12. It's important to note that B12 comes from the microorganisms in the soil and by those in the intestines of animals, ourselves included. It used to naturally be consumed when we would pull our crops fresh from the earth and drink from streams. Plants grown in soil that is rich in B12 have been shown to absorb it. Sadly, most foods are now much more processed and the slew of pesticides, herbicides and other chemicals in the soil & groundwater has been theorized to have killed this natural nutrient; so much so, that most of the animals raised in factory farms and some other smaller operations are fed B12 supplements as well because otherwise they wouldn't get nearly enough of it.[9] So, we can simply take the supplement ourselves or eat foods fortified with it and just cut out the innocent middle animal. Some foods to consume to make sure you get enough B12 include fortified nutritional yeast (some contain up to 600%+ of your needed daily value in just two tablespoons), cereals, plant milks, some vegan yogurts, nori seaweed, plant based meats & tempeh.

The next myth I would like to tackle is that human physiology requires the consumption of flesh and that we cannot get all of our proper nutrients from plants. This is blatantly false.

First, let's look at our intestinal tracts. Herbivores have long intestinal tracts designed to slowly and thoroughly digest plant foods. Carnivores have comparatively shorter digestive tracts meant to quickly pass food through the system so that the flesh doesn't have time to rot & cause illness. Humans have quite a long digestive tract - about 30 feet long in the average adult - and separated into eight main parts.[10]

To deepen the comparison, carnivores' jaws move up and down, allowing them to tear flesh from a body and swallow it whole. Humans, in contrast, can move our jaws both up & down and side to side, allowing us to grind our food into smaller digestible bits. Our molars (back teeth) are flat and square for this purpose. Our canines, which many like to point to as proof that we are carnivores, are tiny and incapable of puncturing through someone's flesh without great effort. Our soft and small fingernails wouldn't be much help to us either. If you look at the *claws* of a predator you will see that they are designed to kill. Ours, simply are not.

Vitamin C is another key indication of our need for plant consumption. Carnivores produce their own vitamin C, humans do not.[10] This means that we need to consume it, and it is only found in plant sources. While we have socially evolved in recent history to consume animal products, our bodies have not. We can eat meat, but most of us don't have to.

Now, some of you may be wondering about protein? What about protein ?! There has been a lot of talk circulating around "complete" protein. What this phrase is referring to is protein sources that contain all nine essential amino acids, which are the building blocks of protein. Our bodies have the capability to make some of them, but the following nine need to be consumed dietarily: histidine, isoleucine, leucine, lysine, methionine, phenylalanine, threonine, tryptophan & valine. Animal products contain all nine of these amino acids, which is why people argue that animal products are essential to our diets; however, the right combination of plants can give us the exact same nutrients without the health deficits caused by eating animals.

Some examples of plant-based foods that have all or nearly all of the amino acids needed to be considered a complete protein include: quinoa, tofu, tempeh, edamame, amaranth, buckwheat, Ezekiel bread, spirulina, hemp seeds, chia seeds and nutritional yeast. Some combos that make up complete proteins include rice & beans, pita & hummus, and a peanut butter and jelly sandwich with whole grain bread.[11] As you can see, it's quite possible to get all of the nutrients you need through plant sources, it just takes a bit more research about what it is you're really eating, which I think everyone could benefit from.

If you are transitioning to this lifestyle and you have any concerns or questions about nutrition, I highly suggest using Cronometer which is both an app and a website. Here you can input the foods you consume on any given day and track your nutrient intake. This way you can raise your awareness about what you may need to shift or balance in your diet. It's great to do this for a good two weeks until you are nutritionally confident. NutrionFacts.org is also another excellent resource for finding information related to human health and plant based living.

Vegans Beware !

Being vegan is much more than just following a plant-based diet. While that is an important aspect of this lifestyle, it's not the only thing you've gotta be aware of. Animal products have snuck their way into clothes, shoes, furniture, make-up, lotions, soaps, art supplies and several other nooks and crannies of our everyday, materialistic lives. A good rule of thumb is to get in the habit of *always* reading the label on everything you buy and doing some research on the companies you support. Here are some keywords to look out for that indicate a product is not vegan:

Food

Casein, butter fat, lactose, whey powder - all derived from dairy

Albumen - egg whites or protein from eggs

Bone Char - literally charred animal bones

Lard - rendered fatty tissues of a pig

Carmine/ Cochineal/ Cochineal extract/ Natural red 4/ E120 / Crimson Lake - boiled & crushed cochineal beetles

Gelatin - boiled skin, tendons, ligaments and sometimes bone

L- Cysteine - derived from feathers

Shellac/ Confectioner's Glaze - made from a resin excreted by the female lac beetle

Mono & Diglycerides - Sometimes derived from animal fat, but other times from plant sources

Vitamin D3 - Often derived from wool, but sometimes derived from Lichen (vegan friendly)

Cosmetics & Hygiene Products

Beeswax - wax created by honeybees

Lanolin - A waxy oil derived from sheep & their wool

Keratin - comes from feather, hair, hooves and horns of animals

Musk - taken from the glands of a male musk deer

Civet - excretions from an african cat-like animal

Castoreum - extracted from the castor sacs of beavers

Kasturi- another secretion from male deers

Pearls - created by oysters, who are usually killed when pearls are extracted

Tallow - rendered from the fat found in the kidneys of cows & sheep

Look for " Cruelty Free" or " No Animal Testing" on labels, if a product doesn't have this than it's likely to have been tested on animals. Also, the cruelty free label does not equate to the product not containing animal products, it just means it wasn't tested on animals.

Apparel & Furniture

Leather - animal skin

Fur, wool, angora, cashmere, down - animal fur/feathers

Silk - typically derived from the bombyx mori moth

Activism

Congratulations! You've made it through the roughest chapters of the book and into the light of change. Activism is an essential foundation of the transformation we are calling forth. In this section I'll be discussing what activism is, how to do it in its many forms, and how to avoid burnout.

What is activism?

Put simply, activism is taking action for a cause. Anyone can be an activist and there is no one "right" way to be an activist. There are many different styles, approaches and methodologies that are all useful in their own way. Here are some of the most common ways you can do so:

Conversations

The everyday interactions we have with people matter. This is probably the easiest & most day to day form of activism. When we are silent in the face of violence we act as enablers for that violence. This is why speaking up when possible is essential. Talk to your friends, family, coworkers and even strangers about animal rights, veganism and activism. Learn to truly listen to what they have to say instead of just speaking at them. Avoid yelling, name-calling or harsh judgment. When we come from a place of compassion, our message is much more likely to be understood and comprehended.

Leafleting

Hand out vegan literature to people on the streets or leave them in bathroom stalls, airplanes, magazines, bulletin boards, ect. You never know who will pick it up and the impact it will have on the reader.

Stickering

There are plenty of stickers available online that can go on stop signs (for legal reasons I am not suggesting that you sticker property that is not yours ;), flesh packaging at grocery stores, and random places around town. Also, if you have a car: sticker it up! Cars are moving billboards and people often read what bumper stickers have to say.

Chalktivism

Write vegan messages on sidewalks with chalk! It can say "go vegan" or "watch (insert vegan doc)" or "ditch dairy."

Social media

Make a video, write a post, share a picture, promote a documentary on Tiktok, Instagram, Facebook, YouTube, ect. You may reach one person or a thousand. A platform of any size is valuable. One thing to note, however, is to avoid becoming an echo chamber. Platforms like Tiktok are specifically nice for avoiding this. On Facebook, for example, if you're only friends with vegans and three family members then that's who you're gonna reach. By expanding your reach and stepping into new territories you have the opportunity to positively influence people you may have never met before.

Photography & Filmography

Taking pictures of animals at sanctuaries, factory farms or outside of slaughterhouses can be incredibly powerful. Most people don't see animals as individuals, so to have them personified in a photo is impactful. Most activist events also appreciate having someone around with a camera to capture the action and share it on social media to gain a bigger audience. On the note of filmography, I personally went vegan because of a documentary. Many people I know did the same. Creating a powerful film documenting the realities of these industries and the power we have to disrupt them is incredible.

Animal rescue

One of the most direct forms of activism involves rescuing animals. This can happen legally, or in a legally questionable fashion. Regardless, someone was saved. Sometimes people willingly surrender their animals and a rescue is fairly simple, other times it involves in-depth planning and an acceptance that you might end up in jail The Animal Liberation Front does rescues in secret and their aim is to liberate as many animals as possible

Open Rescue

Open rescue is the same as rescuing an animal, but being very vocal about it. Direct Action Everywhere specializes in open rescues. The goal of which being to liberate animals, denormalize violence, empower people to take direct action and to challenge and hopefully change the laws in place. I have participated in two open rescues and have been arrested at one of them. To learn more visit directactioneverywhere.com/open-rescue

Vigils

Vigils typically involve standing outside of slaughterhouses to await trucks that will be bringing animals in. The point is to show them love and compassion in their final moments and have any conversations possible with the slaughterhouse workers and passerbys. The Save Movement primarily holds vigils. There are safety concerns involved. Recently, a long time activist was intentionally hit by a truck driver and literally cut in half at a vigil. This is the first time anything like this has been documented, so it is rare, but for this reason I suggest getting involved with The Save Movement as a safety precaution if you'd like to hold or participate in vigils.

Street Activism

There are countless forms of street activism, many of which include holding signs and often footage of animal abuse. My favorite type is what my organization, PEACE, does, as well as Anonymous for the Voiceless. It involves a demonstration where signs are held with a simple message and activists stand in a formation holding footage of animal ag. People on outreach await passersby to stop and engage with the footage, then we step in and ask if they have any questions. The conversations that emerge from these types of events are transformative. Many people have never seen this type of footage before, and afterwards literally thousands of people have pledged to go vegan on spot.

Marches

This type of activism is more rare, but good animal rights marches happen in most major cities annually. It's honestly one of the most enjoyable forms of activism in my opinion purely because of the energy in the crowd and the power in numbers.

Disruptions

The focus of a disruption is to denormalize a system of oppression. Disruptions often involve going into places that are normalizing violence (most restaurants, grocery stores, malls, etc) & protesting what is occurring. They can be silent with the words being on signs or they can be loud and involve chanting or speak outs. This type of activism is very off putting for many people. I would like to offer a perspective on why I still feel it needs to occur. Here is an excerpt of notes I took from a speaker whose name I do not recall at the animal Liberation Conference in 2018 "At one point I attended a seminar on Kinglian non-violence. I thought that what the speaker had to say about this was excellent: " We are not causing conflict. We are trying to hear it. When you walk into a grocery store, the conflict level is overt, yet this conflict is ignored. The purpose of direct action is to bring the tension that already exists to the surface. When we pretend that conflict isn't there we are doing a disservice to everyone and to ourselves. Conflict is inevitable and violence comes from mismanaged conflict." Often, activists will try to assimilate into violent conditions and won't speak up for what they believe in, in order to avoid bringing conflict to the surface. This reminds me of something my women's studies professor once said to me " your silence won't protect you."

Write a book or blog

Writing is empowering. Creating a book to share information with people or a detailed blog post can change lives.

Create educational art

Art is often emotionally impactful for people. There is a specific Instagram account (@barbaradanielsart) that creates images of animal agriculture, if our position with other animals was flipped. She recently released a book titled Dominion over Man. I suggest checking it out.

Volunteer at a sanctuary or start one!

Find a local sanctuary and see if they're accepting volunteers! Sanctuary work can be physically exhausting but is emotionally fueling. Cuddling with Buddy the cow from Iowa Farm Sanctuary has literally swooped me out of peak depression. Last week two pigs named Archie and Ironman rolled over so I could give them belly rubs and I almost cried tears of joy. Additionally, if you have room in your home, land and some serious time on your hands then consider starting a sanctuary! There are some sanctuaries who have 6 roosters and others who have hundreds of animals. Big or small - they're all important.

Transport animals

Oftentimes animals are in need of transport from harmful situations to sanctuaries. Keep an open eye for "free animal" ads and/or join the Emergency Vegan Action Squad on Facebook

Create a vegan business

If you feel called to, form a restaurant, cosmetic line, upcycling company, organic plant farm, or whatever else your heart calls you to do! Providing vegan alternatives to typically non vegan items is needed to help the world transition.

Become a lawmaker or lobbyist

Animals aren't protected by the law because the people exploiting them own the lawmakers. If animal rights activists were holding office then our legal system would look much different. Consider becoming a governor, congressperson, senator or running for president.

Form a Body Blockade/ Lock Down

This is a form of direct action and is usually used as a means to stop something from happening by placing your own body in the way. I've been arrested twice, both for chaining myself to an animal agriculture facility. It was quite effective at completing its intended purpose. I don't recommend doing this unless you're with other people, have a clear (hopefully achievable) goal, and feel confident that you are not in any real danger.

Grow Your Own Food

The generation of people growing the food we eat is dying off, and not many young people are willing to get into the agricultural business. This is why it's so important that the younger generation practice food resilience and heal the land. On one acre of land you can grow enough food to sustain yourself! Food Sovereignty removes your support from industrial agricultural production which is harmful to the planet and the animals who live here. I recently learned that the organic farm run by the university in my town sprays fish bodies on their crops as a fertilizer. I was absolutely disgusted to hear this! In order for our food to be truly cruelty free, I feel we need to know exactly where our food is coming from - and where better than our own yards !

How to Avoid Burnout

Activism, in its many forms, can take its toll. Burnout is common among the activist community and taking time to repair and replenish your heart, mind and body is necessary. I don't say any of this to scare you away from activism because activism is absolutely essential if we are to save our animal kin and ourselves. I say this to be honest and upfront about the weight that this kind of knowledge can have on a person. It is literally a life or death type of situation. Our activism promotes life.

Balance is truly key. You must make time to care for yourself: read a non animal rights book, go on a hike, pick up a new crafty hobby, go to the movies, dance, sing, get a massage, do whatever is life affirming for you. After going to a particularly difficult event such as a vigil or rescue, make sure to rest and mentally check in with yourself. If you have someone that is able to hold space for you then talk to them. Perhaps journal your thoughts and feelings.

Another way is to shake up your activism! You don't have to do the same event every week and you are not required to be constantly posting on social media about animal liberation. Take a break. Rest when necessary. Maybe you went to four vigils in the last couple weeks and now you'd rather do some chalktivism. Take your time. It's better to go to or organize events when you feel energetically capable of doing such things instead of doing everything you possibly can and then burning out for years.

Animal Rights Organizations

The following is a list of animal rights organizations I am familiar with and generally support, as well as, what they do:

The Save Movement - vigils

Direct Action Everywhere - Open Rescue, Disruptions, Community building

Anonymous for the Voiceless - cube of truth (street activism)

Sea Shepherds - badass activists who take to the seas to prevent whaling, illegal fishing and promote veganism

PETA: People For The Ethical Treatment of Animals - street activism, political lobbying, animal rescue, general outreach

Animal Activist Mentorship Program (AAM) - mentor vegans who would like to become activists or be mentored by a vegan activist!

PEACE: Promoting Equality, Acceptance & Compassion Everywhere - street activism, vigils, animal rescue & transport. I include my own group last because we've been fairly inactive the last couple years but I am working to improve that. The other groups are simply more well established

Project Counterglow - A website that contains a map of all known factory farms, slaughterhouses and other animal exploitation facilities in the United States, along with a paper trail of information reported by activists on many of these sites. If you'd like to see what's in your area then this is a fantastic resource.

Expanding Our Sphere of Compassion

Animal rights is a major pillar of social justice and is deeply embedded in the web of oppression that seems to be present just about everywhere. Once you have a clear understanding of the animal rights movement, I strongly encourage you to look into other liberatory movements. The oppression of our fellow humans is prominent just about everywhere and runs deeper than many of us are aware. When you're ready, below is a list of documentaries & websites to investigate in order to gain a greater perspective on some of the issues we face and the proposed solutions.

- **Stopline3.org:** Line 3 is an oil pipeline extension carrying tar sands (one of the worst kinds of fossil fuels) from Alberta, Canada to Superior, Wisconsin. This pipeline crosses previously untouched wetlands, treaty territory of the Anishinaabe peoples and crosses the Mississippi River several times. This is especially detrimental due to the company's history with oil spills and the fact that the Mississippi River is a major water supply for many people in this nation. Indigenous people have been fighting this pipeline since 2014 when it was first proposed since it violates their treaty rights and poses a massive threat to their homeland and the environment as a whole. Unfortunately, despite years of protests & direct action, the oil pipeline became operational on October 8th of 2021.

- **The 13th:** The prison system of the United States stands as a way for those in power to legally enslave humans. A majority of which are people of color. There are people in jail right now, serving years for the "crime" of smoking weed. There are people who were wrongfully accused of more serious crimes such as murder, and have faced the death penalty for something they didn't even do. Yes, there are also those who did what they were jailed for doing. The question to ask, I feel, is who do jails really serve? Do they genuinely protect people? Do they improve the mental state and overall well being of those inside? Do they make the world a safer place to be? For the most part, I would argue no. For a deeper understanding, watch The 13th on Netflix

- **Black Lives Matter:** Born from the unjust killing or Trayvon Martin and the acquittal of his murderer & amplified by the protests that followed the murder of Michael Brown, Black Lives Matter has become a global organization and social justice movement focused on the true liberation of Black people. I suggest browsing their website and listening to their podcast "Imagining Abolition."

- **Climate Justice:** Our planet has endured years of literal bombings, oil spills, degradation and utter disrespect from billions of us. A few specific entities (corporations & governments) make up a humongous percentage of this damage and need to be held accountable for their actions. One way we as individuals can work to hold these businesses accountable is to boycott their products when possible and support those that are helping the planet. We can also vote in legislators who vow to pass laws that will uphold these values and protest when necessary. Another way is by becoming as self-sufficient as possible. Growing food indoors & outdoors, composting, upcycling, creating eco-bricks, building rain-water catchment systems and planting literal seeds in our communities are some ways to do this. It's incredibly empowering to rely less on the industries that wreak havoc on our planet and to see the direct result of your wholesome lifestyle.

- **The Trevor Project:** To quote their website, " The Trevor Project is the world's largest suicide prevention and crisis intervention organization for lesbian, gay, bisexual, transgender, queer, and questioning (LGBTQ) young people." A wealth of educational resources are provided on their website, along with 24/7 access to counselors and the ability to connect to an international community of young LGBTQ people.

Peaceful Recipes for a Healthy Planet

The Basics

AVOCADO TOAST

*Ingredients * for 1 serving * :*

- 1 Slice of Bread
- ½ Avocado
- 2 dashes of Salt & pepper
- 1 dash of lemon & lime juice
- Sprinkle of nutritional yeast

Directions:

1. Toast 1 slice of bread
2. Cut & mash ½ an avocado in a bowl until the texture is smooth
3. Mix in the salt, pepper, lime & lemon juice
4. Spread the avocado mix onto toast
5. Gently sprinkle nutritional yeast on top
6. Enjoy with love!

BLACK BEANS

Ingredients:

- 6 cups water
- 2 cups black beans
- Salt

Directions:

1. Rinse and sort dry black beans. Remove split beans or stones while saying positive affirmations to yourself
2. Soak the beans overnight in water, using a 1 cup beans to 2 cups water ratio
3. In the morning, drain and rinse beans

4. Next, add the beans to a pot and cover in water, making sure there's 3 or so inches of water above the beans, add a few dashes of salt
5. Bring the pot to a boil, then reduce heat to a simmer and cover
6. Monitor the water level periodically as the beans cook, they should take about 60-80 minutes
7. Taste them around this time mark to ensure if they're ready or not
8. When done, either store the beans in a container in the fridge or transfer them straight to the dish you're preparing :)

CAULIFLOWER CHEESE

Ingredients:

- 1 cauliflower
- 1/2 carrot
- 1 cup of vegetable broth
- ½ cup nutritional yeast
- ½ stick of veggie butter
- ½ tsp pepper
- ½ tsp cumin
- 2 tsp salt
- 1 tsp garlic powder

Directions:

1. Bring a large pot of water to a boil
2. Chop the cauliflower & carrots into small pieces
3. Add the chopped veggies to the boiling water, set timer for 20 mins
4. Once done, strain the veggies and add all ingredients into a blender
5. Blend !!!!
6. Congrats you did the thing! Thanks for being awesome!

CASHEW CHEESE

Ingredients:

- 1 cup cashews
- 5 tbsp tapioca starch
- 1 ½ cup veggie broth
- 1 can full fat coconut milk
- ½ tsp pepper
- ½ tsp cumin
- 2 tsp salt
- 1 tsp garlic powder

Instructions:

1. Boil cashews for 18 minutes or soak for 30-40 minutes in hot water, drain when done
2. Combine all ingredients into a blender and do a thorough blend !! Make sure there are no cashew chunks floatin around
3. After blending, pour the mix into a pan and turn the heat on medium-high
4. Once it starts bubbling, stir the cheese around with a spatula or stirring stick of your choice until the texture is thicc and sticky
5. You did it!! Taste the cheese & add seasoning as deemed necessary.

BROWN RICE

Ingredients:

- 4 cups of water
- 2 cups of brown rice
- 2 teaspoons olive oil
- Love

Directions:

1. Rinse rice in a strainer

2. Combine all ingredients in a pot, bring to boil
3. Cover, reduce the heat & simmer for 45 minutes
4. Remove from heat and let it sit covered for 10 more minutes
5. Fluff with a fork and affirmations of well being
6. Alternatively, you can cook it in a rice cooker

HOLY GUACAMOLE

Ingredients:

- 1 avocado
- 3(ish) tablespoons of salsa
- Salt, pepper & garlic powder to taste
- 1 squirt lemon juice & lime juice

Directions:

1. Cut & carefully pit one avocado
2. Smoosh it with a fork
3. Add all seasonings and do a good mixin
4. This dish is flexible due to avocados being different sizes, so the last step (which is taste it) is really important to ensure that the seasonings are adequate

OAT FLOUR

Ingredients:

- oats

Directions:

1. Love yourself
2. Blend oats
3. You did it ! nice!

REFRIED BEANS

Ingredients:

- 2 cups of pinto or black beans
- 8-10 cups of water
- 2 tbsp oil
- 1 tablespoon lime juice
- 2 teaspoons cumin
- 2 teaspoons garlic powder

- 2 teaspoons of onion powder
- 3 teaspoons of salt
- 2 teaspoons of pepper
- 1 teaspoon oregano

Directions:

1. Pour the beans into a large bowl, then remove and discard any beans that are split or shriveled and any small rocks
2. Fully cover the beans with water in a pot, making sure there's about 3-4 inches of water on top of them, then set on the counter to soak overnight (or for 8 hours minimum)
3. The following morning, drain and rinse the beans under cool water
4. Transfer them to a large pot and add about 8-10 cups of water and a few dashes of salt
5. Bring the beans to a boil, then reduce the heat to a low simmer. Cover and cook for 2-3 hours, periodically checking in and giving them a little stir. If they begin to foam then the heat is on too high
6. At hour 2, check the beans to see if they're ready. They should be firm, but easy to bite through. If they're at all crunchy then give them more time to cook
7. Once finished, remove from heat and strain
8. Pour into a large pan with about two tablespoons of olive oil and mash, add about ¼ to ½ a cup of water and continue mixin and mashin
9. Add all seasonings and mix
10. Taste your brilliance and make adjustments as needed

TOFU

Ingredients:

- 1 package tofu
- ¼ (ish) cup olive oil
- 1 teaspoon salt
- ½ teaspoon pepper
- 1 teaspoon garlic powder
- ½ teaspoon cumin
- 1 tablespoon tamari

Directions:

1. Drain 1 package of tofu and then cut it into cubes, strips of small triangles
2. Fill the bottom of a large pan with olive oil and add in the tofu, cook on medium-high heat (ALTERNATIVE: use an air fryer! Start by putting the cut up tofu on the pan, then add in a little bit of oil, tamari and a good layer of all the seasonings. Mix it all together then put in the air fryer and cook for 15 minutes, flip the tofu and cook for another 5-10 ! This is my favorite method since it requires a fraction of the oil I usually use)
3. *back to the pan fry method* Once it begins to crisp (make sure to monitor it!) then add in a few dashes of tamari, salt, pepper, cumin & garlic powder

4. Consistently stir it around while still giving it enough time to get crispy. We typically cook our tofu until they're a crisp brown on each side, however you can cook them to your preference!
5. This process generally takes between 10-20 minutes
6. Enjoy !! (ps. I often prep a block of tofu, keep it in the refrigerator and then when I'm hungry sometimes I just munch on it cold. I think it's really good!)

WHITE RICE

Ingredients:

- 2 cups white rice
- 2 cups water

Directions:

1. Rinse the rice in a colander until the water runs clear
2. Combine the rice & water in a medium saucepan over medium-high heat & bring to a boil, uncovered
3. Reduce the heat to low & cover, cook for 15 minutes
4. Remove from heat and let stand for 10 minutes
5. Youuuuu did it!

Plant Favorites

BLACK BEAN QUEEN

Ingredients:

- 1 cup rinsed & chopped kale
- ½ cup brown rice
- ½ cup black beans
- 1 scoop (about 2 tablespoons) guacamole
- Drizzle of cauliflower cheese

Directions

1. Gather ingredients and ensure that they're ready for immediate use (prepared rice, beans, cauliflower cheese & guacamole is required for this dish)
2. Place one cup of chopped kale in a bowl
3. Add ½ cup of cooked brown rice on top
4. Then add ½ cup of seasoned black beans
5. Take 1 big spoonful of guacamole and place it in the middle
6. Lightly drizzle cauliflower cheese over this royal dish
7. Give yourself thanks because you just made a nutritious and delicious meal :)

MAC & PLANTCHEESE

Ingredients:

- Brown rice noodles (or noodles of choice)
- 1 cauliflower
- 1 carrot
- ½ cup of vegetable broth
- ½ cup water
- ½ cup nutritional yeast
- ½ stick of veggie butter
- 2 teaspoons pepper
- 3 teaspoons salt
- 1 teaspoon garlic powder

Directions:

1. Bring a large pot of water to a boil
2. Chop the cauliflower & carrots into small pieces
3. Add the chopped veggies to the boiling water, set timer for 20 mins
4. Bring another large pot of water to a boil, then add in noodles and cook for 16 minutes (or the time the package instructs)
5. In a blender, add all other ingredients and do a good blend
6. Strain the veggies when done & add to the mixture
7. Blend until creamy!!!!

8. Strain the noodles when the time is up & then put them back in the now empty pot (off of the previously hot stove), then fill with caulicheese and mix it all together!

9. Send gratitude to everyone involved with the creation of this life-giving meal, including you!

SHROOMWITCH

Ingredients:

- Two pieces of organic bread
- ¼ - ½ cup uncooked sliced mushrooms
- 2 tbsp olive oil
- 1/2 tbsp tamari
- Salt & pepper to taste
- 1 good piece of lettuce
- Two slices of a tomato
- ½ an avocado
- 1 tbsp veganaise

Directions:

1. Splash a bit of olive oil on a pan and bring to medium heat, add the mushrooms

2. Once the mushies start sizzling add the tamari, salt, pepper and a little bit more oil

3. Cook until the mushies are crispy and smell irresistible
4. As the mushies cook, place two pieces of bread into a toaster
5. Once toasted, spread the veganaise onto one of the pieces of bread, then spread the avocado on the other
6. Put two slices of a tomato on top of the veganaise, then cover it with a good rinsed leaf of lettuce, then add the mushrooms
7. Sandwich all the deliciousness together, cut it in half and enjoy with love

MEGA TOTS

Ingredients:

- 5 potatoes
- 1 cup of uncooked rice
- 1 bell pepper
- ½ stick of vegan butter
- 1 cup quick oats
- 2 tbsp nutritional yeast
- 1 tsp garlic powder
- ¾ teaspoon black pepper
- 1 tsp salt
- 3 tbsp oil

Directions:

1. Preheat oven to 420

2. Cook 1 cup of brown or white rice

3. Fill a large pot a little more than half the way up with water and bring to a boil

4. As the water heats up, wash the potatoes

5. Cut the skin of the potato off and collect in a bowl. I recommend using a knife and not being too conservative with cutting off a bit of the inside too because we'll be making chips with them (option, don't cut the skins off for chips and instead just chop the potato as a whole)

6. Once the potato is skinless, chop into 4-8 pieces

7. Repeat this process with all the potatoes

8. Once the water is boiling, put the potatoes (not the skins) in the water and set a timer for 15 minutes

9. Now for the chips, add about 3 tablespoons of your choice of oil to the bowl and a nice layer of seasonings (I suggest salt, pepper & garlic powder)

10. Using your hand, mix it all together so that all the chips are nicely coated in oil and seasoning

11. Spread on a baking sheet and place in the oven for 15 minutes, then flip and bake for another 10

12. While the potatoes are baking, wash & chop the bell pepper into small pieces and then cook in a pan with a little bit of oil for 5-8 minutes, stirring occasionally

13. Once the potatoes are done boiling, poke them with a fork to make sure they're soft and mashable. If they are, then dump them in a strainer in the sink (the pot handles will likely be hot so wear oven mitts !)

14. Turn off the stove and place the pot back on it, then add in ½ stick of butter and the cooked rice

15. Allow the butter to mostly melt, then add in the potatoes & seasoning

16. Mash & mix it all together, then add in 1 cup of quick cook oats and the cooked bell pepper

17. Mix it all up!

18. Option to place the mixture into the refrigerator for 20 or so minutes to allow it to cool, but it's not necessary

19. Next, put parchment paper on either the bottom of an airfryer (if you don't have one I highly recommend getting one if you can, it's my favorite kitchen gadget) or a baking sheet

20. Roll up the mashed potato mixture into balls about the size of a golf ball and place on the sheet, then lightly sprinkle salt on top of them

21. bake/air fry for 15 minutes, then with tongs roll them over so the other side can crispify too and allow them to cook for 10-15 more minutes

22. Repeat this process with the rest of your material & enjoy the potato chips you just made !

23. Ketchup & vegan ranch make great condiments for this dish and optional add ins for the mash include: jalapenos, mushrooms, broccoli and vegan cheese

PASTA ROYALE

Ingredients:

- Fettuccine brown rice noodles
- ½ cup uncooked sliced mushrooms
- 1 yellow squash

- 1 cup chopped kale
- 1 cauliflower
- 1 small carrot
- ½ cup of vegetable broth
- ½ cup water
- ½ cup nutritional yeast
- ½ stick of veggie butter
- 2 teaspoons pepper
- 3 teaspoons salt
- 1 teaspoon garlic powder

Directions:

1. Bring a large pot of water to a boil
2. Chop the cauliflower & carrot into small pieces
3. Add the chopped veggies to the boiling water, set timer for 20 mins
4. Bring another large pot of water to a boil, then add in noodles and cook for 16 minutes (or instructed time)
5. thinly slice the squash & kale
6. Splash some olive oil on a pan and heat it on medium-high, add in sliced mushrooms
7. Once the mushrooms start sizzling, add ½ tablespoon of tamari and a few dashes of salt & pepper
8. Cook until the mushrooms are beginning to crispy, then add squash & kale - cook until they're looking divine (about 3 minutes)
9. In a blender, add all other ingredients and do a good blend
10. Strain the cauliflower & carrots when done boiling & add to the mixture
11. Blend !!!!

12. Strain the noodles when the time is up & then put them back in the now empty pot, then fill with caulicheese and veggies & mix it all together!
13. Acknowledge the divine being that you are & enjoy!

OH MY STIR FRY

Ingredients (for a large batch):

- 5 cups brown rice
- 1 sliced squash
- 6 chopped stalks of asparagus
- 1 cup sliced mushrooms
- 1 cup cubed tofu
- 1 ½ cups chopped kale
- ½ cup sliced bell pepper
- 3(ish) tablespoons tamari
- Garlic powder, salt & pepper to taste

Directions:

- Cook brown rice (see instructions under the brown rice tab)
- Drain 1 package of tofu before slicing in half and cubing
- Add to a pan with olive oil on medium-high heat (or air fry it for 10-15 minutes)
- While the tofu is sizzling, begin to slice the mushrooms

- In the same pan as the tofu, add the mushrooms & 1 tbsp tamari
- Monitor as they cook, making sure that they don't burn while still getting crisp
- As they continue to cook, slice/chop the asparagus, kale, bell peppers & squash - once the tofu & mushrooms look fairly crisp, add in all other ingredients (besides rice), turn heat down a bit and cover
- After allowing to sit for a minute or two, add seasonings and stir
- Once all veggies look ready, add in the brown rice and mix it all together with some more tamari
- Taste when you believe you are done and add seasoning as needed
- The individual serving size is 2 cups of joy

SUSHI LOVE BOWL

Ingredients:

- 1 ½ cups white rice
- Tamari (as needed)
- 1/4th cup chopped tofu
- 1/4th cup sliced mushrooms
- 1 scoop of tofutti cream cheese
- 1/4th a sheet of seaweed crumbled as garnish
- 1/2 an avocado
- Salt, pepper, garlic powder & cumin to taste

Directions:

- Cook white rice (see instructions)
- Drain & chop 1/4th cup of tofu and cook in a pan with olive oil, salt, pepper & garlic powder (or air fry for 10-15 minutes)
- Once the tofu has begun crisping up a bit, add in sliced mushrooms and some tamari
- As they're cooking, take 1 ½ cups of white rice and add it into a separate pan with some tamari and a tiny dash of oil, fry it up
- Once the rice looks lovely, pour it into a bowl and check on the tofu/shrooms - once they're crispy, add em too
- The tofu & mushrooms should fill about half the side of the bowl, on the other side carefully add the avocado and a scoop of cream cheese
- Next, artistically crumble 1/4th a sheet of seaweed overtop the dish and set an intention with the meal: love, laughter, nourishment, well-being & peace

PLANT TACOS

Ingredients (for mix):

- 2 cups refried beans
- 1 cup chopped cauliflower (optional)
- ½ cup brown rice

- Salt, pepper, cumin, garlic powder to taste

(toppings ~ for 3 tacos)

- ⅓ cup sliced mushrooms
- ⅓ cup thinly sliced bell peppers
- 3 tablespoons sour cream (1 per taco)
- 3 tablespoons salsa (1 per taco)
- ⅓ cup guacamole (evenly divided)
- ½ cup of chopped lettuce (evenly divided)
- 3 corn taco shells

Directions:

1. First, see if refried beans are prepped and if not, then begin cookin some beans (canned works too). Do the same with the brown rice.
2. Create the core mixture
3. Chop 1 cup of cauliflower & fry with olive oil, salt, pepper & garlic powder
4. Once the cauliflower is crispy, add in the brown rice and continue cooking
5. Next, add the refried beans and continue cooking
6. You did the thing!
7. Slice mushrooms & bell peppers, then add to a separate pan with olive oil, tamari, a dash of salt, pepper, cumin & garlic powder
8. Cook until crispy, then add to a bowl
9. Using the same pan (adds flavor to the taco shells), add a bit more oil if it's looking dry, and place three taco shells in the pan, with half of the shell directly on the pan and half of it on the side.

This makes it so that the middle part of the shell cooks nicely and doesn't break down the middle

10. Add a large spoonful of the mix onto each of the shells, then add a spoonful of the mushroom/bell pepper mix on top

11. Using a spatula, flip the tacos over so that they're in more of a taco form and make sure they cook evenly on both sides

12. Once crispy, take the tacos off of the pan and onto a plate

13. Apply the sour cream, guac, salsa and then lettuce to the inside of the tacos

14. Bless them with love and gratitude

TOFU SCRAMBLE ON AVOGODDESS TOAST

Ingredients:

- 1 Slice of Bread
- ½ Avocado
- Salt & pepper
- 1 dash of lemon juice
- 1/4th cup cubed tofu
- 8 slices of bell peppers
- 8 slices of mushrooms (approx)
- Olive oil

Directions:

1. Cube 1/4th cup of tofu & cook with olive oil, salt & pepper (or air fry for 10 minutes)
2. In a separate pan (unless tofu is precooked), cook the sliced mushrooms until beginning to crisp, then add in bell peppers - once done, take off heat
3. While the food is cooking, toast 1 slice of bread
4. Mush ½ an avocado until the texture is smooth & mix in lemon juice
5. Spread the avocado mix onto the toast
6. Top with the tofu scramble and enjoy with gratitude

BROCCOLI HEARTZOTTO

Ingredients:

- 1 Cauliflower
- ½ stick veggie butter
- 1 cup veggie broth
- ½ cup nutritional yeast
- 1 teaspoon pepper
- 2-3 teaspoons salt
- 1 teaspoon garlic powder

- ½ teaspoon cumin
- 1 large head of broccoli (or more depending on how much you like)
- 5-6 cups of cooked brown rice

Instructions:

1. Cook 3 cups of brown rice (see Brown Rice if confused)
2. Bring a large pot of water to a boil
3. Wash & chop cauliflower to small pieces
4. When the water is boiling, add in the cauliflower and cook for about 20 minutes (or until the cauliflower is soft and blendable)
5. While the cauliflower boils, wash and chop the broccoli into small bits as well
6. In a pan, add a dash of oil and about a cup or so of water along with the broccoli. Put a lid overtop and steam on medium-high heat
7. Monitor the broccoli closely & when the texture is still firm but easy to cut through then remove from heat. By now the water should have evaporated, if not then pour it out.
8. Once the cauliflower is done, strain and add into a blender
9. Add veggie broth & butter, nutritional yeast & seasonings into the blender as well and blend it all until smooth
10. Add the cheese mix into the large pan with the cauliflower (or a pot if the pan isn't big enough) and mix together, then add the rice one cup at a time while stirring
11. Once all is combined, give it a taste! If all is well then enjoy! If it needs more seasoning then sprinkle in salt, pepper, garlic powder and any other seasoning you feel is fitting until you're satisfied !
12. Enjoy!

INFINITY BOWL

Ingredients:

- ½ cup chopped kale
- ½ cup chopped lettuce
- ½ cup cooked black beans
- ½ cup cooked brown rice
- ¼ cup sliced mushrooms
- 1 heaping spoonful of refried beans
- 1 heaping spoonful of guacamole
- 1 heaping spoonful of sour cream
- 1 tbsp sprouts
- ½ tbs tamari
- Salt, pepper, garlic powder to taste
- Dash of olive oil

Directions:

1. Gather ingredients, ensure that the black and refried beans are precooked, as well as the brown rice, if not then get to prepping
2. Slice ¼ cups worth of mushrooms (ideally shiitake) and cook in olive oil, a little tamari, salt and pepper on medium-high until crispy
3. In a different pan, mix black & refried beans with rice and cooked on medium until nice and warm

4. As the mixture is cookin, prepare the lettuce & kale and add it to the base of a bowl (make sure to wash them first)
5. Prepare guacamole (see the guac page)
6. Once all is cooked, add the bean and rice mixture overtop the greens and then top with mushies
7. Take a scoop of guac and sour cream and place them on top, then garnish with sprouts n love

BREAKFAST BURRITO

Ingredients:

- 1 large tortilla
- ½ cup refried beans
- ¼ cup tofu
- 1/2 small potato
- 1/3 bell pepper
- ½ cup spinach
- ½ cup mushrooms
- 1 tbsp Tamari
- 2 whopping scoops of guacamole
- Salt, pepper, garlic powder, cumin, nutritional yeast to taste

Directions:

1. Cube tofu and put into a pan with a bit of olive oil, tamari and a dash of salt, pepper & garlic powder
2. Either cook the tofu on medium-high heat for 10-15 minutes of air fry it for the same amount of time
3. Next, cube and cook the potato in the same manner (minus the tamari). You can also air fry them together!
4. Slice mushrooms & add into a separate pan with olive oil, a little tamari, and a few dashes of salt, peper, garlic powder & cumin. After about 5 minutes, add in bell pepper, then the spinach
5. Warm up refried beans
6. Prepare the guacamole (see guac page)
7. When everything is finished cooking, take the veggies out of the pan and use it to warm up the tortilla
8. Give it about 5-15 seconds on each side, then move it to a plate
9. Put the beans on the center base of the tortilla, then the veggie mixture over that (option: add guacamole inside now if you plan to eat it with your hands or outside if you intend to eat it with a fork & knife)
10. Fold the edges of the tortilla inwards as much as is comfortable (so that they're almost touching), then use your thumbs to press the tortilla side nearest to you inward towards the filling and roll it into a burrito
11. This meal is excellent to enjoy right away or to save it for later & pan fry it in a little bit of oil when you're ready to devour

SPAGHETTI TACOS

Ingredients:

- 1 package spaghetti
- 1 can marinara sauce
- Nutritional yeast
- ⅕ stick vegan butter
- Olive oil
- Soft taco shells
- Optional: beyond meat, guacamole, vegan sour cream

Instructions:

1. Cook spaghetti per instructions on the box
2. If you'd like to, then cook beyond meat patties simultaneously. Cut them up into pieces with your spatula and cooked for about 7-10 minutes while stirring around occasionally
3. Once the noodles are finished, strain them and add into a pot with marinara sauce and vegan butter
4. Get out a pan (or use the one you used for the veggie meat) and add some olive oil, turn up the heat to medium high
5. Place three tortillas on the pan with half of the shell on the bottom of the pan and the other half on the side. This allows one side to cook, as well as the middle.

6. Place a couple forkfuls of spaghetti on each of the tortillas (on the pan side), then sprinkle some nutritional yeast on top of that and add some of the veggie meat if you chose to cook that

7. After about 3-5 minutes (depending on how hot the pan has gotten) flip the pan side of the tortillas up to sandwich the spaghetti in between the other side of the tortilla, then let the side that has not been cooking to cook for about the same amount of time

8. Ideally each side will be a golden brown by the time they've finished, you may have to flip them back and forth a bit to ensure equal cooking

9. Once done, remove from the pan and add vegan sour cream and guacamole if ya'd like to!

10. This recipe makes a ton of spaghetti tacos, so it's great for a party!

SUPER SALAD

Ingredients:

- ½ cup lettuce
- ½ cup kale
- ½ cup spinach
- 1/5th of a cucumber sliced
- ½ sliced avocado
- Shredded tiny carrot
- Optional: ¼ cup chopped mushrooms

- Dressing of choice (recommended is Annie's Goddess dressing or a big glob of your favorite hummus)

Instructions:

1. Gather all ingredients and chop those that need it
2. If you'd like to, cook the mushrooms on medium-high heat with salt, pepper, garlic powder and a splash of tamari until crispy. As you're doing this:
3. Mix the lettuce, kale and spinach at the base of the bowl
4. Add the cucumber and avocado on top of that
5. Top with dressing and shredded carrots
6. Add the mushrooms on top of it all
7. Have yourself a good time

THE NUTRIKING

Ingredients:

- 1/2 cup cauliflower cheese
- 1 cup black beans
- 1 cup refried beans
- 1 cup brown rice
- 1 big spoonful of guacamole
- 1/2 cup of cubed tofu
- 1/2 cup sliced mushrooms
- 3 pinches of sprouts
- Salt, pepper, garlic powder, cumin to taste
- Dash of tamari

Instructions:

1. This dish includes a lot of foods that need to be prepared beforehand. Go to the pages in this book that have already instructed how to do so for the: black beans, refried beans, brown rice, tofu, guacamole & cauliflower cheese
2. Great! Once you've done that, in one pot combine 1 cup of black beans, 1 cup of refried beans and 1 cup of brown rice with a splash of tamari and a sprinkle of salt, pepper, garlic powder and cumin
3. Mix it all together and heat on medium with a little oil
4. Simultaneously, warm up about ½ cup of cauliflower cheese
5. While those are getting steamy, begin cooking about ½ cup of mushrooms in olive oil, tamari, garlic powder, salt, pepper and cumin on medium-high in a pan
6. After about five minutes, add ½ cup of pre cooked tofu with the mushrooms to warm it up
7. Cooked for about 3-5 more minutes

8. Once the bean mixture is all warm, place it all in a bowl
9. Cover half of the bean mix with cauliflower cheese
10. Cover the over half of the mix with tofu & mushrooms
11. Take a big spoonful of guacamole and place it in the middle of the dish
12. Create a crown of sprouts along the outer edge of the bowl
13. Freaking enjoy you king!

NACHO ROYALE

Ingredients:

- 1 cup of cauliflower cheese
- 1 plate or bowl full of chips
- 1 cup of precooked black beans
- ¼ sliced bell pepper
- ½ cup pre cooked tofu
- 1 pinch of sprouts
- Big scoop of guacamole

Instructions:

1. This dish requires a bit of prep, so make sure you have cauliflower cheese, black beans, tofu and guacamole prepared!
2. Now that you've got that sorted, slice and cube your bell pepper
3. Cook in a pan on medium heat with some olive oil, salt and cumin

4. After about four minutes, add in the pre cooked tofu
5. Give it another couple minutes, then add in the black beans
6. Cooked for about 5 minutes altogether while heating up the cauliflower cheese in a different pan
7. While they heat up, create a small mountain of chips on either a plate or big bowl
8. Once the cheese is all warm, drizzle it on top of the chips
9. Spread out the bean mixture overtop of that
10. Follow it up with a big scoop of guac in the middle
11. Garnish with sprouts lightly atop the whole thing
12. Delish!

CHICKPEA OF THE SEA

Ingredients:

- Two cups of cooked chickpeas
- 2 tbsp veganaise
- 4 tbsp relish
- A good leaf of lettuce or a small handful of spinach

- 2 slices of bread
- A few squirts of lemon juice
- Salt, pepper, garlic powder & nutritional yeast to taste

Instructions:

1. First things first, you gotta cook ya beans. If your using canned precooked chickpeas you can skip the next couple steps
2. Using about a cup and a half of chickpeas (you can use more if you'd like to have a lot of the mixture to save) sort and rinse the chickpeas. Pick out any rocks that may have gotten in there or shriveled chickpeas
3. Soak for 8 hours or overnight OR bring a big pot of water to a boil with the chickpeas in, allow to boil for 5-10 minutes then remove from heat
4. Cover the pot with a lid and allow them to sit for about an hour
5. After either method, strain and rinse the chickpeas
6. Next, add the beans to a large pot and cover with several inches of water, bring it all to a boil then reduce the heat to a simmer
7. Cover with the lid slightly ajar
8. Cook for about 2 hours, stirring on occasion and checking the texture after hour two. You want them to be easily smooshable
9. Once they've cooked fully, pour them into a strainer and then a bowl
10. This next part is most easily done with an electric hand mixer but can be done with a big fork or whisk or your hand with much more effort: Mash all the chickpeas
11. When everything is thoroughly smooshed, (for about 2 cups of chickpeas) add a spoonful of veganaise and two spoonfuls of rel-

ish. Mix in. At this point, add in a bit more veganaise or relish as needed for texture

12. For flavor, add in about 3-4 squirts of lemon juice, a good layer or salt, pepper, garlic powder and nutritional yeast

13. Mix it all together

14. Taste and adjust as needed

15. Once the mixture is done, toast your slices of bread!

16. When toasted, lightly spread veganaise on one side and relish on the other

17. Add a leaf of lettuce to one side of the bread and a couple good scoops of the mixture on top of it

18. Make it as thicc or thin as you'd like and finish the sandwitch by placing the other piece of bread on top of the mixture

19. Enjoy!

SAVORY SOUP

Ingredients:

- Water
- 1 1/2 cups of black beans
- 2 stocks of sliced celery
- 1 chopped carrot
- 1 cubed red potato
- ½ pack of cubed tofu
- 3 leafs of finely chopped kale

- 1 box of vegetable broth
- 1 teaspoon thyme
- 1 teaspoon oregano
- 2 teaspoon salt
- 1 teaspoon pepper
- 2 teaspoons garlic powder
- 1 teaspoon cumin

Directions:

1. Rinse and sort dry black beans. Remove split beans or stones while saying positive affirmations to yourself
2. Soak the beans overnight in water, using a 1 cup beans to 2 cups water ratio
3. In the morning, drain and rinse beans
4. Next, add the beans to a pot and cover in water, add a few dashes of salt
5. Bring the pot to a boil, then reduce heat to a simmer and cover
6. Monitor the water level periodically as the beans cook, allow to cook for about 20 minutes
7. Chop & cube all other ingredients, then add into the soup & allow to simmer for 40-60 minutes
8. While adding in the veggies, also add in the vegetable broth & a good layer of all of the seasonings. Stir well
9. Periodically check on ya soup, when everything is soupy enough for you then remove from the heat, pour into a bowl and enjoy!

GRILLED CHEESE

Ingredients:

- 1 cup boiled cashews
- 5 tbsp tapioca starch
- 1 ½ cup veggie broth
- 1 can full fat coconut milk
- Salt, pepper, garlic powder to taste
- Olive oil or vegan butter
- Bread!
- Optional: vegan breakfast patty, sliced mushrooms, vegan burger pattie, sliced vegan sausage

Instructions:

1. Boil cashews for 18 minutes, drain when done
2. all ingredients into a blender and do a thorough blend !! Make sure there are no cashew chunks floatin around
3. After blending, pour the mix into a pan and turn the heat on medium-high
4. Once it starts bubbling, stir the cheese around with a spatula or stirring stick of your choice until the texture is thick and sticky. Season to taste and stick it in the fridge overnight. This cheese needs to cool down significantly to get to the right texture for grilled cheese. Put in a bowl and let cool in the fridge overnight. This cheese amount will be enough for 3-5 sandwiches

5. This sandwitch is really delicious with cooked mushrooms or vegan meat alternatives, so if you'd like to add those in then cook them now!

6. Next, butter the pan or put light olive oil on it and lay down two slices of bread on the pan, cook on medium heat

7. Let the sides cook for a couple minutes then flip over, add cheese on one of the sides and top with the vegan meat alternative if ya have it

8. Sandwich the other slice of bread on top of the cheese side and grill for a couple minutes

9. Flip and cook for a couple minutes on the other side as well

10. Once cooked to your satisfaction, take off the pan, slice & enjoy!

11. This grilled cheese is served delicious with tomato soup & potato wedges!

Sweets

WAFFLES

Ingredients:

- 4 bananas
- 3 cups oat flour
- 1.5 cups plant milk
- 3 tablespoons of sugar
- 2 teaspoons baking soda

- 3 dashes cinnamon
- 1 teaspoon vanilla
- 3/4 cups chocolate chips
- A little vegan butter

Directions:

1. Hi gorgeous, you're adding so much joy into the world. Plug in the waffle iron :)
2. While still in their peels, give the 4 bananas a good mushin
3. Unpeel the mushy goodness and empty the bananas into a large bowl.
4. Add in cinnamon, vanilla & baking soda and mix it all together until smooth
5. Add in the plant milk & stir in the oat flour 1 cup at a time, then stir in the chocolate chips
6. Butter both sides of the iron & then place about 1 ⅓ cups of the batter in the center of the iron and spread it around a bit
7. Close & flip the iron and cook for 2-3 minutes
8. Carefully remove the waffle from the pan with tongs or fork and place on a plate, artistically decorate the waffle with the chosen toppings (my favorite is strawberries & whip cream)
9. Give yourself a little hug cause you did great

FRENCH TOAST

Ingredients:

- A loaf of sliced bread
- 1 tbs Just egg
- 3 dashes of cinnamon
- 1 tbsp maple syrup
- ¼ cup of vanilla Plant milk
- optional toppings: maple syrup, powdered sugar, strawberries, whip cream

Instructions:

1. Combine the just egg, cinnamon and vanilla plant milk in a medium sized bowl
2. Mix thoroughly

3. Have a pan prepared on the side, set on medium heat and butter the bottom of the pan

4. Quickly dip the bread into the mixture, ensuring its fully covered, then put the bread onto the pan, continue this process until no more bread can fit on the pan

5. Allow the bread to cook on one side for about 3-5 minutes, then flip! Allow to cook for the same amount of time on the other side or until golden brown, then remove them from heat onto a plate

6. Serve with maple syrup and/or fruit toppings!

CREATOR COOKIES

Ingredients:

- 4 bananas
- 3 cups oat flour
- 2 cups oat milk
- 1 cup oats (lol)
- 3 tablespoons of (brown or white) sugar
- 2 teaspoons baking soda
- 3 dashes cinnamon
- 1 teaspoon vanilla
- 3/4 cups chocolate chips

Directions:

- Preheat the oven to 375

- While still in their peels, give the 4 bananas a good mushin
- Unpeel the mushy goodness and empty the bananas into a large bowl
- Add in cinnamon, vanilla & baking soda and mix it all together until smooth
- Add in the oat milk & stir in the oat flour 1 cup at a time, then stir in the oats & chocolate chips
- Line a cookie sheet with parchment paper, place 8 balls of cookie dough on the sheet, bake for 16 minutes with love and care

MANGO NICECREAM

Ingredients:

- ½ frozen mango
- ½ frozen banana

- ¼ cup plant milk
- Optional toppings: fruit, granola, chia seeds

Instructions:

1. Gather ingredients and add them all to a powerful blender
2. Allow to sit and defrost for about 2 minutes, then blend them all together
3. Once smooth & creamy, add any topping of choice & enjoy!

JOYFUEL

Ingredients:

- 1 ½ frozen bananas
- 2 cups of chocolate plant milk
- 1 heaping scoop of peanut butter
- Optional: 1 tablespoon of cacao
- Optional: 1 tbsp protein powder
- Optional: 1 tbsp chia seeds
- Optional: vegan whip cream

Instructions:

1. Freeze unpeeled bananas broken into smaller pieces overnight

2. The next day, combine all ingredients into a blender
3. Allow the mix to sit for a minute or two to give the banana an opportunity to dethaw a little bit
4. Blend until smooth & enjoy!

MAGICK MATCHA FRAP

Ingredients:

- 1 tablespoon of Matcha powder
- 1-2 tablespoons of maple syrup
- 1 ½ cups of plant milk
- 3-6 plant milk ice cubes
- Dash of pure vanilla extract

Instructions:

1. Pre-make plant milk ice cubes
2. Add all ingredients into a blender
3. Blend until smooth(ish)
4. Enjoy!

I hope that you find pleasure in crafting these recipes! Feel free to be creative and make alterations as you see fit, and take inspiration wherever you may find it. If you feel so inclined to add any of these recipes to the menu at a restaurant, café or food service then please know you have my full approval. I would love to see these meals spread across the world and give life to those who consume them.

Epilogue

Whew! We did it! I wrote it, you read it! We did that!!

This book has been both a pleasure and a pain to create, as much of the wealth of information I gathered was quite new to my noggin. My original plan to just quickly create a recipe book evolved into this collection of knowledge. I dearly hope that the information, thoughts & feelings I have relayed in this book has a profound impact on you, the reader, and the communities you are a part of. Each and every one of us has the potential to heal this planet, ourselves and our loved ones.

We are powerful beings, and our actions do not go unnoticed. We, the people, make up the governments, corporations, work force and families that inhabit this world. By choosing compassion, we generate a ripple of change that extends far beyond our awareness. It may touch people we have never even met who have the power to make legislative or business decisions that could impact millions. Your actions matter, and I hope that this book has empowered you to embody that sentiment. I know it has done so for me.

I would like to once again bring us back to the first questions I asked of you in the prologue:

How do you value life?
What does your life mean to you?
How do you determine the value of life?

Personally, my life means a great deal to me. Every day I feel honored to be here. I give gratitude to my vessel and feel lucky to be able to experience all that I do. I like to assume that others feel similarly about their lives as well. Many of us were born without any memories of before and a profound wonder for what comes after. Truly, we don't know until we know, which makes being present in the moment that much more important. I don't know what's after this life. I am excited to find out, but for now I am deeply grateful for the gift of life I get to experience.

I feel blessed to be able to write these words and have you read them. Sometimes the vibrant, richness of life is so exquisite that I literally sing about it, often while giggling. This kind of ecstatic joy is something I wish for all beings. I feel that everyone on this planet (and beyond) deserves to feel happy and to feel free. When valuing the life of another, I assume that their value is equal to my own. Their experiences have likely been vastly different, their perceptions are a mystery to me, but I feel that their life is sacred. I feel that all our lives are sacred, and I do what I can to honor that.

So, beloved, you are a sacred spark of creation and from the deepest part of my being, I thank you for being present with me now. I appreciate each and every one of you who have and continue to support the momentum of peace on this planet. Please share what you have learned with your loved ones, research and investigate any questions that may have arised, get active in your area & reach out to me about any inquiries or collaborations you may have in mind.

With love, I thank you for being.

& I leave you with these happy images of animals living their best life.

Sources

My Journey To Veganism

1. The Vegan Society. 2021. Definition of veganism. [online] Available at: <https://www.vegansociety.com/go-vegan/definition-veganism

The Reality Of Animal Agriculture

1. Manes, C. (2010). *CAFO (concentrated animal feeding operation): The tragedy of industrial animal factories.* Page 27. San Rafael, CA: Earth Aware.
2. Zampa, M. and Zampa, M., 2019. 99% of U.S. Farmed Animals Live on Factory Farms. [online] Sentient Media. Available at: <https://sentientmedia.org/u-s-farmed-animals-live-on-factory-farms/ >

3. Kimbrell, A. (2010). *CAFO (concentrated animal feeding operation): The tragedy of industrial animal factories.* Page 18. San Rafael, CA: Earth Aware

4. Rollin, B. (2010). *CAFO (concentrated animal feeding operation): The tragedy of industrial animal factories.* Pages 6 & 7. San Rafael, CA: Earth Aware.

5. Imhoff, D. (2010). *CAFO (concentrated animal feeding operation): The tragedy of industrial animal factories.* Page 39. San Rafael, CA: Earth Aware.

Fish

1. Zampa, M., n.d. How Many Animals Are Killed for Food Every Day?. [online] Sentient Media. Available at: <https://sentient-media.org/how-many-animals-are-killed-for-food-every-day/>

2. Fish Pictures & Facts. (2012). Retrieved from https://www.nationalgeographic.com/animals/fish

3. Brown, C., 2015. [online] Wellbeingintlstudiesrepository.org. Available at: <https://www.wellbeingintlstudiesrepository.org/cgi/viewcontent.cgi?article=1074&context=acwp_asie>

4. Jab, F., 2018. It's Official: Fish Feel Pain. [online] Smithsonian Magazine. Available at: <https://www.smithsonianmag.com/science-nature/fish-feel-pain-180967764/>

5. Lingel, G., Fish Farming: Harming Oceans While Poisoning People and the Environment. [online] Sentient Media. Available at: <https://sentientmedia.org/fish-farming/>

6. Finney, C., 2018. Why is caviar still on the menu?. [online] the Guardian. Available at: <https://www.theguardian.com/food/2019/oct/16/why-is-caviar-still-on-the-menu>

7. Attenborough, D. (Director). (2019). *Our Planet* [Video file]. Retrieved from https://www.netflix.com/title/80049832

8. Rollin, B. (2010). *CAFO (concentrated animal feeding operation): The tragedy of industrial animal factories.* Page 8. San Rafael, CA: Earth Aware.

9. SECORE International: Why coral reefs need our help. (n.d.). Retrieved from https://www.secore.org/site/corals/detail/why-coral-reefs-need-our-help.23.html

10. Oceanservice.noaa.gov. n.d. How much oxygen comes from the ocean?. [online] Available at: <https://oceanservice.noaa.gov/facts/ocean-oxygen.html>

11. Schauber, G., 2017. Cows, Pigs, and Poultry – The Leading Cause of Ocean Dead Zones? – news and views on ocean conservation. [online] Blogs.ubc.ca. Available at: <https://blogs.ubc.ca/making-waves/2017/02/07/cows-pigs-and-poultry-the-leading-cause-of-ocean-dead-zones/>

12. Sabine, C., n.d. Carbon Dioxide in the Ocean and Atmosphere - sea, depth, oceans, important, system, plants, marine, oxygen, human. [online] Waterencyclopedia.com. Available at: <http://www.waterencyclopedia.com/Bi-Ca/Carbon-Dioxide-in-the-Ocean-and-Atmosphere.html>

13. Roach, J. (2021, May 04). Seafood May Be Gone by 2048, Study Says. Retrieved from https://www.nationalgeographic.com/animals/article/seafood-biodiversity

Bycatch

1. Zampa, M., 2018. How Many Animals Are Killed for Food Every Day?. [online] Sentient Media. Available at: <https://sentient-media.org/how-many-animals-are-killed-for-food-every-day/>

Whales

1. Breyer, M. (2020, October 19). 11 Facts About Blue Whales, the Largest Animals Ever on Earth. Retrieved from https://www.treehugger.com/facts-about-blue-whales-largest-animals-ever-known-earth-4858813
2. Whale & Dolphin Conservation USA. n.d. Information and facts about whaling - Whale & Dolphin Conservation USA. [online] Available at: <https://us.whales.org/our-4-goals/stop-whaling/>
3. Sea Shepherd Conservation Society. 2021. Sea Shepherd Welcomes the End of Whaling in the Southern Ocean. [online] Available at: <https://seashepherd.org/news/sea-shepherd-welcomes-the-end-of-whaling-in-the-southern-ocean/>
4. "Save Lolita: Raising Awareness for Lolita the Orca." Save Lolita , www.savelolita.org/.

Dolphins

1. Facts About Dolphin Captivity. (n.d.). Retrieved from https://www.dolphinproject.com/campaigns/captivity-industry/facts-about-captivity/
2. Psihoyos, Louie, director. The Cove. 2009.
3. Whale & Dolphin Conservation USA. n.d. Information and facts about whaling - Whale & Dolphin Conservation USA. [online] Available at: <https://us.whales.org/our-4-goals/stop-whaling/>
4. "Read 'Dolphins and the Tuna Industry' at NAP.edu." National Academies Press: OpenBook, 1992, www.nap.edu/read/1983/chapter/2.

5. Tabrizi, Ali, director. Seaspiracy . 2021.
6. Fiorillo, J. (2021, March 29). Dolphin Safe group alleges 'Seaspiracy' left out critical details from the executive's interview. Retrieved from https://www.intrafish.com/tuna/dolphin-safe-group-alleges-seaspiracy-left-out-critical-details-from-executives-interview/2-1-989370

Sharks

1. The Ocean Portal Team Reviewed by David Shiffman. (2019, October 16). Sharks. Retrieved from https://ocean.si.edu/ocean-life/sharks-rays/sharks
2. Ariansyah, Sumardi, and Karli Thomas. "10 Little-Known Shark Facts." Greenpeace USA, 16 July 2020, www.greenpeace.org/usa/10-little-known-shark-facts/.
3. "Shark Finning and Fin Facts." Shark Stewards, 24 Apr. 2021, sharkstewards.org/shark-finning/shark-finning-fin-facts/.
4. Threats to Sharks - Overfishing. (n.d.). Retrieved from http://www.supportoursharks.com/en/conservation/Threats_to_sharks/Overfishing.htm#Anchor

Lobsters

1. Lobsters and Crabs Used for Food. (2020, September 26). Retrieved from https://www.peta.org/issues/animals-used-for-food/factory-farming/fish/lobsters-crabs/

Cows

1. "Cows." Animal Facts - Cows, www.veganpeace.com/animal_facts/Cows.htm.
2. Ostlind, E. (2011, March 21). The Big Four Meatpackers. Retrieved from https://www.hcn.org/issues/43.5/cattlemen-struggle-against-giant-meatpackers-and-economic-squeezes/the-big-four-meatpackers-1
3. Sanders, B. (2018, October 09). Global Cow Slaughter Statistics and Charts. Retrieved from https://faunalytics.org/global-cow-slaughter-statistics-and-charts/
4. Pollan, M. (2010). *CAFO (concentrated animal feeding operation): The tragedy of industrial animal factories.* Pages 53-58 San Rafael, CA: Earth Aware.
5. The Rape Rack. (2016, June 20). Retrieved from https://their-turn.net/2016/06/15/2016061420160613the-rape-rack/
6. Newkey-Burden, Chas. "Dairy Is Scary. The Public Are Waking up to the Darkest Part of Farming | Chas Newkey-Burden." The Guardian, Guardian News and Media, 30 Mar. 2017, www.theguardian.com/commentisfree/2017/mar/30/dairy-scary-public-farming-calves-pens-alternatives.

7. Imhoff, D. (2010). *CAFO (concentrated animal feeding operation): The tragedy of industrial animal factories*. Pages 152 & 154. San Rafael, CA: Earth Aware.

8. "The Truth About The Dairy Industry." Animal Equality | International Animal Protection Organization, 27 May 2020, animalequality.org/issues/dairy/.

9. Craig Thomas, Michigan State University Extension. "Drinking Water for Dairy Cattle: Part 1." MSU Extension, 20 Sept. 2018, www.canr.msu.edu/news/drinking_water_for_dairy_cattle_part_1.

10. 1 in 3 people globally do not have access to safe drinking water – UNICEF, WHO. (n.d.). Retrieved from https://www.who.int/news/item/18-06-2019-1-in-3-people-globally-do-not-have-access-to-safe-drinking-water-unicef-who

11. "Rodeos: Inherent Cruelty to Animals." The Humane Society Veterinary Medical Association, www.hsvma.org/rodeos_inherent_cruelty_to_animals.

12. Larson, P. (n.d.). Animal Abuse Inherent in Rodeo. Retrieved from https://sharkonline.org/index.php/rodeo-veterinarian-speaks-out

13. The Animal Reader, et al. "Spain Starts Killing 1600 Calves after Months at Sea on the Elbeik." The Animal Reader, 25 Mar. 2021, www.theanimalreader.com/2021/03/25/spain-starts-killing-1600-calves-after-months-at-sea-on-the-elbeik/

Goats

1. "Goats for Meat and Dairy." Goats for Meat and Dairy – Woodstock Sanctuary, woodstocksanctuary.org/learn/animals-used-for-food/goats-for-food/.
2. Author: Bas Sanders | Published: October 10, et al. "Global Goat Slaughter Statistics and Charts." Faunalytics, 4 Oct. 2018, faunalytics.org/global-goat-slaughter-statistics-and-charts/.
3. YouTube/ Goat Milk - The Ethical Alternative, Earthling Ed, 27 July 2020, youtu.be/GUXGTaOZfzg
4. "Broken Shovels Farm Sanctuary: Commerce City, Colorado." Broken Shovels Farm, 22 July 2020, brokenshovels.com/.

Pigs

1. "The Joy of Pigs ~ Pig Facts." PBS, Public Broadcasting Service, 3 Mar. 2021, www.pbs.org/wnet/nature/the-joy-of-pigs-smart-clean-and-lean/2126/.

2. The Vegan, M. (Director). (2021). *Man Exposes Shocking Pig Feed Source in Viral TikTok* [Video file]. Retrieved from https://www.youtube.com/watch?v=9DY70yxWC5A&ab_channel=MictheVegan

3. "Pigs: Intelligent Animals Suffering on Farms and in Slaughterhouses." PETA, 31 Jan. 2021, www.peta.org/issues/animals-used-for-food/animals-used-food-factsheets/pigs-intelligent-animals-suffering-factory-farms-slaughterhouses/.

4. Rollin, B. (2010). *CAFO (concentrated animal feeding operation): The tragedy of industrial animal factories.* Page 5. San Rafael, CA: Earth Aware.

5. Scully, M.. (2010). *CAFO (concentrated animal feeding operation): The tragedy of industrial animal factories.* Page 14. San Rafael, CA: Earth Aware.

6. Greenwald, Glenn. "Hidden Video and Whistleblower Reveal Gruesome Mass-Extermination Method for Iowa Pigs Amid Pandemic." The Intercept, 29 May 2020, theintercept.com/2020/05/29/pigs-factory-farms-ventilation-shutdown-coronavirus/.

7. "Unseen – A Look into the Final Hours of Life for Pigs from Smithfield." YouTube, 15 July 2020, youtu.be/b_Weq4iZQ48.

8. AVMA Guidelines for the Depopulation of Animals: 2019 Edition. (2019). Page 45. Retrieved from https://www.avma.org/sites/default/files/resources/AVMA-Guidelines-for-the-Depopulation-of-Animals.pdf

9. Gruber-Miller, S. (2021, April 13). Iowa Legislature sends another 'ag gag' bill criminalizing specific types of trespass to Gov. Kim

Reynolds. Retrieved from https://www.desmoinesregister.com/story/news/politics/2021/04/12/iowa-legislature-passes-new-ag-gag-agriculture-trespass-bill-governor-kim-reynolds/7099951002/

Chickens

1. Briggs, H. (2018, December 12). 'Planet of the chickens': How the bird took over the world. Retrieved from https://www.bbc.com/news/science-environment-46506184

2. (2017, December 21). 17 Chicken Facts the Industry Doesn't Want You to Know. Retrieved from https://freefromharm.org/animalagriculture/chicken-facts-industry-doesnt-want-know/

3. Berkhout, N., & McDougal, T. (2013, June 20). Study suggests chickens are smarter than toddlers. Retrieved from https://www.poultryworld.net/Meat/Articles/2013/6/Study-suggest-chickens-are-smarter-than-toddlers-1289715W/

4. The Chicken Industry. (2016, June 30). Retrieved from https://www.peta.org/issues/animals-used-for-food/factory-farming/chickens/chicken-industry/

5. Imhoff, D. (2010). *CAFO (concentrated animal feeding operation): The tragedy of industrial animal factories.* Pages 39, 160 & 168. San Rafael, CA: Earth Aware.

6. How are chickens slaughtered and processed for meat? (2020, October 02). Retrieved from https://www.chickencheck.in/faq/how-chickens-slaughtered-processed/

7. "Egg Farming: Facts and Truth About the Egg Industry." Million Dollar Vegan, 27 Aug. 2020, www.milliondollarvegan.com/egg-farming/.

8. Watt, H. (2018, June 19). How much does big pharma make from animal antibiotics? Retrieved from https://www.the-guardian.com/environment/2018/jun/19/how-much-does-big-pharma-make-from-animal-antibiotics

9. Poultry vaccines. (2021, January 21). Retrieved from https://vete-riankey.com/poultry-vaccines/

10. Cucker, B. (2020, June 26). To help prevent pandemics, stop eating meat. Retrieved from https://www.earthday.org/to-prevent-pandemics-stop-eating-meat/

11. "How to Decipher Egg Carton Labels." The Humane Society of the United States, www.humanesociety.org/resources/how-decipher-egg-carton-labels.

12. Parsons, R. (2021, May 13). 10 Things to Love About Chickens. Retrieved from https://www.onegreenplanet.org/animalsandnature/things-to-love-about-chickens/

13. Trauth, Erin. "What Those Food Labels Really Mean: 'Free Range,' 'Cage Free,' and 'Grass Fed'." One Green Planet, One Green Planet, 8 Jan. 2014, www.onegreenplanet.org/vegan-food/what-those-food-labels-really-mean-free-range-cage-free-and-grass-fed/.

14. "Why Don't Vegans Eat Backyard Eggs?" SURGE, www.surgeactivism.org/backyardeggs.

15. Bakalar, N. (2019, March 15). Are Eggs Bad for Your Heart Health? Maybe. Retrieved from https://www.nytimes.com/2019/03/15/well/eat/eggs-cholesterol-heart-health.html

He is just body.

16. McGarry, J. (2018, October 02). Safe storage of eggs. Retrieved from https://www.canr.msu.edu/news/safe_storage_of_eggs

17. Greger M.D. FACLM on March 26th, Michael. "Peeks Behind the Egg Industry Curtain." NutritionFacts.org, 26 Mar. 2015, nutritionfacts.org/2015/03/26/peeks-behind-the-egg-industry-curtain/.

Turkeys

1. "10 Turkey Facts." World Animal Protection, 28 Sept. 2020, www.worldanimalprotection.us/blogs/10-turkey-facts.

2. Girczyc, Christine. "The Curiosity, Intelligence, and Personality of Turkeys." Animal Outlook, 18 June 2020, animaloutlook.org/personality-turkeys/.

3. "Editorial: There's a Grim Reality behind Your Thanksgiving Turkey." Los Angeles Times, Los Angeles Times, 22 Nov. 2017, www.latimes.com/opinion/editorials/la-ed-turkey-slaughter-20171122-story.html.

4. "9 Things The Turkey Industry Doesn't Want You to Know." Animal Equality | International Animal Protection Organization, 2 Mar. 2020, animalequality.org/blog/2019/11/27/turkey-industry-cruelty/.

5. "The Turkey Industry." PETA, 7 Nov. 2018, www.peta.org/issues/animals-used-for-food/factory-farming/turkeys/turkey-industry/.

Ducks & Geese

1. Interesting facts about ducks: Just Fun Facts. (2020, June 07). Retrieved from http://justfunfacts.com/interesting-facts-about-ducks/

2. 10 Facts about Geese. (2019, April 09). Retrieved from https://www.four-paws.org/campaigns-topics/topics/farm-animals/10-facts-about-geese

3. "Reichardt Duck Farm Exposed." YouTube, Direct Action Everywhere, 6 Feb. 2021, youtu.be/HhYYrur9ORQ.

4. YouTube, Condition One, 6 June 2019, youtu.be/Vr95Hir8bzw.

5. Code Section 597e. (2020). Retrieved from https://leginfo.legislature.ca.gov/faces/codes_displaySection.xhtml?lawCode=PEN§ionNum

6. Duck Farm: How Are Ducks Farmed And How Long Do Ducks Live? (n.d.). Retrieved from https://thehumaneleague.org/article/duck-farm

7. "Birds Plucked Alive on Farms Linked to 'Responsible' Down Suppliers." YouTube, 26 May 2016, youtu.be/dqS5dX2DpwY.

8. Foie Gras: Cruelty to Ducks and Geese. (2020, December 21). Retrieved from https://www.peta.org/issues/animals-used-for-food/factory-farming/ducks-geese/foie-gras/

9. "The Duck and Goose Meat Industry." PETA, 14 Oct. 2013, www.peta.org/issues/animals-used-for-food/factory-farming/ducks-geese/ducks-goose-meat-industry/

Sheep

1. 10 surprising facts about sheep! (2020, August 11). Retrieved from https://spca.bc.ca/news/facts-about-sheep/

2. Biology Behind Homosexuality In Sheep, Study Confirms. (2004, March 09). Retrieved from https://www.sciencedaily.com/releases/2004/03/040309073256.htm

3. "The Wool Industry." PETA, 12 Jan. 2021, www.peta.org/issues/animals-used-for-clothing/wool-industry/.

4. "The Top 5 Countries With the Most Sheep." Top 5 of Anything Brand Image, top5ofanything.com/list/d4d1ef5e/Countries-With-the-Most-Sheep.

5. "16 Reasons To Stop Wearing Wool: Animal Liberation Victoria." 16 Reasons To Stop Wearing Wool | Animal Liberation Victoria | Fighting for Animal Rights, www.alv.org.au/sheep-truth/16-reasons-to-stop-wearing-wool/.

6. "Exposed: Lambs Mutilated, Sheep Kicked and Hit With Electric Clippers on Argentine Wool Farm." PETA Exposés and Undercover Investigations, 7 Dec. 2020, investigations.peta.org/argentine-wool-farm-lambs-mutilated-exposed/.

7. "Sheep for Meat and Wool." Sheep for Meat and Wool – Woodstock Sanctuary, woodstocksanctuary.org/sheep/.

8. Lambs & Sheep: Animal Liberation Victoria. (n.d.). Retrieved from https://www.alv.org.au/the-facts/issues/lambs-and-sheep/

Horses

1. Bradford, Alina. "Mustangs: Facts about America's 'Wild' Horses." LiveScience, Purch, 4 May 2021, www.livescience.com/27686-mustangs.html.

2. Forrest, Susanna. "The Troubled History of Horse Meat in America." The Atlantic, Atlantic Media Company, 8 June 2017, www.theatlantic.com/technology/archive/2017/06/horse-meat/529665/.

3. "Horse Slaughter." ASPCA, www.aspca.org/animal-cruelty/horse-slaughter.

4. Rodriguez, C. (2013, February 23). We Have All Eaten Horse, Like It or Not. Retrieved from https://www.forbes.com/sites/ceciliarodriguez/2013/02/23/we-have-all-eaten-horse-like-it-or-not/?sh=31c9b0a33617

5. "Horse Racing Exposed: Drugs & Death." PETA, support.peta.org/page/2587/action/1?locale=en-US.

6. Nonprofit offers alternative to slaughter for Amish horses. (2005). Retrieved from https://www.cleveland19.com/story/3349105/nonprofit-offers-alternative-to-slaughter-for-amish-horses/

7. "Rodeos Are Animal Abuse, Not Entertainment." Farm Animals Facts & News by World Animal Foundation, www.worldanimalfoundation.com/advocate/farm-animals/params/post/1280920/rodeos-are-animal-abuse-not-entertainment.

Rabbits

1. Living in Harmony With Wild Rabbits. (2019, January 08). Retrieved from https://www.peta.org/issues/wildlife/rabbits/

2. "Rabbits." NAL, www.nal.usda.gov/afsic/rabbits.

3. Murray, Loraine. Encyclopædia Britannica, Encyclopædia Britannica, Inc., www.britannica.com/explore/savingearth/rabbits-the-poster-child-for-animal-rights.

4. "Why Rabbits Need Your Help Perhaps More Than Any Other Animal." PETA, 27 Sept. 2019, www.peta.org/features/rabbits-need-help/.

5. How Whole Foods' Bunnies Are Killed. rabbit.org/how-whole-foods-bunnies-are-killed/.

6. Inside the Fur Industry: Factory Farms. (2021, January 13). Retrieved from https://www.peta.org/issues/animals-used-for-clothing/animals-used-clothing-factsheets/inside-fur-industry-factory-farms/

7. Daly, N. (2021, May 03). Here's why Easter Is bad for bunnies. Retrieved from https://www.nationalgeographic.com/animals/article/rabbits-easter-animal-welfare-pets-rescue-bunnies

Foxes

1. Red and Gray Foxes. (2021, June 03). Retrieved from https://www.wildliferescueleague.org/animals/foxes-red-and-gray/

2. PETSAMI. (2013, May 17). A Fox Steals A Man's Golf Ball And Has The Time Of His Life! Retrieved from https://www.youtube.com/watch?v=ul_fxYUgurg&ab_channel=WaggleTV

3. "10 Fascinating Facts About Foxes (With Photos)." PETA UK, 15 Feb. 2019, www.peta.org.uk/blog/10-fascinating-facts-about-foxes-with-photos/.

4. Patterson, L. (2017, August 11). Foxes use magnetic fields to find prey: Earth. Retrieved from https://earthsky.org/earth/foxes-use-earths-magnetic-field-to-jump-on-prey/

5. Mythbusting: The Facts about Fox Hunting." RSPCA, www.rspca.org.uk/getinvolved/campaign/hunting/facts.

6. "EXPOSED: Undercover Investigation at Fur Farm Shows the Lives behind the Label." The Humane Society of the United States, www.humanesociety.org/news/exposed-undercover-investigation-fur-farm-shows-lives-behind-label.

7. "Inside the Fur Industry: Factory Farms." PETA, 13 Jan. 2021, www.peta.org/issues/animals-used-for-clothing/animals-used-clothing-factsheets/inside-fur-industry-factory-farms/

Mink

1. Bradford, Alina. "Facts About Minks." LiveScience, Purch, 13 Sept. 2016, www.livescience.com/56071-mink-facts.html.
2. North Carolina Wildlife Research Commission. (n.d.). Mink. Retrieved from https://www.ncwildlife.org/Learning/Species/Mammals/Mink
3. "Mink Farming: Fur Commission USA." Fur Commission USA | Valuable Accurate Accessible Information about Mink Farming, 19 Feb. 2016, furcommission.com/mink-farming-2/.
4. "Zimbal Mink." YouTube, 2 Dec. 2014, youtu.be/WwPsStvktks.
5. "Mink Farming: Facts, Figures, Statistics." Truth About Fur, www.truthaboutfur.com/en/mink-farming.
6. Animal Ethics. (2020, December 15). Fur farms. Retrieved from https://www.animal-ethics.org/animals-used-for-clothing-introduction/fur-farms/

Rats & Mice

1. "Mice and Rats in Laboratories." PETA, 25 Jan. 2021, www.peta.org/issues/animals-used-for-experimentation/animals-laboratories/mice-rats-laboratories/.
2. "Estimating Mouse and Rat Use in American Laboratories by Extrapolation from Animal Welfare Act-Regulated Species." Nature News, Nature Publishing Group, 12 Jan. 2021, www.nature.com/articles/s41598-020-79961-0

3. David GrimmJan. 12. "How Many Mice and Rats Are Used in U.S. Labs? Controversial Study Says More than 100 Million." Science, 15 Jan. 2021, www.sciencemag.org/news/2021/01/how-many-mice-and-rats-are-used-us-labs-controversial-study-says-more-100-million.

4. "Mice and Rats." American Anti-Vivisection Society, aavs.org/animals-science/animals-used/mice-rats/.

Nonhuman Primates

1. Hall of Human Origin. (n.d.). What Do Primates Have in Common? Humans & Our Cousins: AMNH. https://www.amnh.org/exhibitions/permanent/human-origins/understanding-our-past/living-primates

2. Fobar, Rachel. "Monkeys Still Forced to Pick Coconuts in Thailand Despite Controversy." Animals, National Geographic, 4 May 2021, www.nationalgeographic.com/animals/article/monkey-labor-continues-in-thailands-coconut-market

3. Mott, M. (2021, May 03). The Perils of Keeping Monkeys as Pets. Retrieved from https://www.nationalgeographic.com/animals/article/news-monkeys-primates-pets-trade-ethics

4. Brunette, M. (2019, May 28). The Ugly Business Behind the Bushmeat Trade. Retrieved from https://janegoodall.ca/our-stories/bushmeat-trade/

5. "Primates in Laboratories." PETA, 10 May 2021, www.peta.org/issues/animals-used-for-experimentation/primates-laboratories/.

6. "The Use of Monkeys in Research." RSPCA, www.rspca.org.uk/adviceandwelfare/laboratory/primates.

7. Zhang, S "America Is Running Low on a Crucial Resource for COVID-19 Vaccines." The Atlantic, Atlantic Media Company, 31 Aug. 2020, www.theatlantic.com/science/archive/2020/08/america-facing-monkey-shortage/615799/.

Dogs

1. "23 Amazing Facts About Dogs You Probably Didn't Know." The Drake Center For Veterinary Care, 7 Jan. 2021, www.thedrakecenter.com/services/dogs/blog/23-amazing-facts-about-dogs-you-probably-didnt-know.

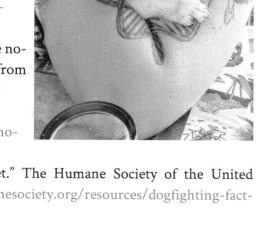

2. "Pet Statistics." ASPCA, www.aspca.org/animal-homelessness/shelter-intake-and-surrender/pet-statistics

3. What does it mean to be no-kill? (n.d.). Retrieved from https://www.animalhumanesociety.org/news/what-does-it-mean-be-no-kill

4. "Dogfighting Fact Sheet." The Humane Society of the United States, www.humanesociety.org/resources/dogfighting-fact-sheet.

5. Daly, Natasha. "Traditional Hunting Dogs Are Left to Die En Masse in Spain." Animals, National Geographic, 3 May 2021, www.nationalgeographic.com/animals/article/spanish-galgo-hunting-dog-killing-welfare.

6. "Hound Dumping: Here's How Hunters Leave Their Dogs to Die." PETA, 9 Dec. 2019, www.peta.org/blog/hound-dumping-hunters-kill-own-dogs/.

7. "Dogs." American Anti-Vivisection Society, aavs.org/animals-science/animals-used/dogs/.

8. Pepelko, Kristina. "The Ugly Truth Revealed: Racing Greyhounds Bled Out in Australia." One Green Planet, One Green Planet, 8 May 2019, www.onegreenplanet.org/news/the-ugly-truth-revealed-racing-greyhounds-bled-out-in-australia/.

9. Iditarod dog kennel horrors. (n.d.). Retrieved from https://help-sleddogs.org/iditarod-dog-kennel-horrors-extreme-neglect-and-dog-abuse/

10. Paws. (n.d.). Buyer Beware: The Problem with Puppy Mills and Backyard Breeders. Retrieved from https://www.paws.org/resources/puppy-mills/

11. What Countries Eat Dogs 2021, worldpopulationreview.com/country-rankings/what-countries-eat-dogs.

12. "Dog Meat Trade." Humane Society International, 24 May 2021, www.hsi.org/issues/dog-meat-trade/.

Cats

"25 Crazy Cat Facts." Assisi Animal Health, 11 Mar. 2020, assisianimalhealth.com/blog/cat-facts/.

"Cats in Laboratories." PETA, 29 July 2019, www.peta.org/issues/animals-used-for-experimentation/cats-laboratories/.

3. Rosenwald, Michael. "The Disturbing History of Cat Abuse: Public Hangings, Pipe Beatings and 'The Great Cat Massacre'." The Washington Post, WP Company, 12 June 2020, www.washingtonpost.com/news/retropolis/wp/2017/06/23/the-disturbing-history-of-cat-abuse-public-hangings-pipe-beatings-and-the-great-cat-r

4. "Cat Fatalities and Secrecy in U.S. Pounds and Shelters." Alley Cat Allies, www.alleycat.org/resources/cat-fatalities-and-secrecy-in-u-s-pounds-and-shelters/.

5. "Dog Meat Trade." Humane Society International, 24 May 2021, www.hsi.org/issues/dog-meat-trade/.

Deer

1. "30 Incredible Facts About the Deer." Conserve Energy Future, 3 May 2020, www.conserve-energy-future.com/facts-about-deer.php.

2. Dobric, M. (2020). 30 Surprising Deer Accidents Statistics. Retrieved from https://petpedia.co/deer-accidents-statistics/

3. "Hunting." PETA, 11 July 2019, www.peta.org/issues/animals-in-entertainment/cruel-sports/hunting/.

4. Chorney, Saryn. "Here's Why You Should Skip the Reindeer Displays and Visit a Real Herd Instead This Christmas." PEOPLE.com, 11 Dec. 2018, people.com/pets/reindeer-displays-christmas-welfare-herd-scotland-cairngorms/.

Wolves, Coyotes, Cougars & Bears

1. The USDA's War on Wildlife. (n.d.). Retrieved from https://www.predatordefense.org/USDA.htm
2. The Humane Society Of The United States. (2015). Wildlife Disservice: The USDA Wildlife Services' Inefficient and Inhumane Wildlife Damage Management Program. Retrieved from https://www.humanesociety.org/sites/default/files/docs/2015-wildlife-service-white-paper.pdf
3. Wolf Facts. (n.d.). Retrieved from http://www.wolfmatters.org/wolf-facts.html
4. "Wolf Reintroduction Changes Ecosystem in Yellowstone." Yellowstone National Park, 20 Mar. 2021, www.yellowstonepark.com/things-to-do/wildlife/wolf-reintroduction-changes-ecosystem/.
5. Infographic: Wolves Keep Yellowstone in the Balance. (2021, March 08). Retrieved from https://earthjustice.org/features/infographic-wolves-keep-yellowstone-in-the-balance
6. "Wisconsin Hunters Kill 216 Wolves in Less than 60 Hours, Sparking Uproar." The Guardian, Guardian News and Media, 3 Mar. 2021, www.theguardian.com/us-news/2021/mar/03/wisconsin-hunters-kill-216-wolves-less-than-60-hours-uproar.
7. Machemer, T. (2021, May 10). New Idaho Law Allows Killing of 90 Percent of State's Wolves. Retrieved from https://www.smith-

sonianmag.com/smart-news/new-idaho-law-allows-killing-90-percent-states-wolves-180977691/

8. Bradford, A., & Pester, P. (2021, April 02). Coyotes: Facts about the wily members of the Canidae family. Retrieved from https://www.livescience.com/27976-coyotes.html

9. Worrall, Simon. "How the Most Hated Animal in America Outwitted Us All." Animals, National Geographic, 3 May 2021, www.nationalgeographic.com/animals/article/coyote-america-dan-flores-history-science.

10. Bruegger, S. (2021, May 18). Time to terminate wildlife killing contests. Retrieved from https://www.registerguard.com/story/opinion/columns/2021/05/18/guest-view-time-terminate-wildlife-killing-contests/5130786001/

11. Cochrane, L. (2021, June 24). Canada Goose fashion brand to stop using fur by the end of 2022. Retrieved from https://www.the-guardian.com/world/2021/jun/24/canada-goose-fashion-brand-to-stop-using-fur-by-end-of-2022

12. "Cougar." Animal Fact Guide, 28 Dec. 2020, animalfactguide.com/animal-facts/cougar/.

13. Mountain Lion Foundation Frequently Asked Questions. (n.d.). Retrieved from https://mountainlion.org/about-mountain-lions/frequently-asked-questions/

14. "Bears, Facts and Information." Animals, www.nationalgeographic.com/animals/mammals/facts/bears-grizzly-polar-panda.

15. Emma. (2021, June 10). How Many Bear Attacks Happen Per Year? [Bear Attack Stats & Facts]. Retrieved from https://paw-someadvice.com/wild/how-many-bear-attacks-per-year/

16. Five Things You Need to Know about Bear Bile Farming. www.animalsasia.org/us/media/news/news-archive/five-things-you-need-to-know-about-bear-bile-farming.html.

Trophy Hunting

1. Why Hunting Enables Poaching. (2021). Retrieved 16 June 2021, from https://medium.com/@unpopularscience/why-hunting-enables-poaching-c8b01c499bc4

2. 8 Trophy Hunting Facts That Will Make You Scream. (2021). Retrieved 16 June 2021, from https://www.worldanimalprotection.us/blogs/trophy-hunting-facts

3. Banning Trophy Hunting. (2021). Retrieved 16 June 2021, from https://www.humanesociety.org/all-our-fights/banning-trophy-hunting

Exotic Animal Trade

1. Fighting illicit wildlife trafficking: A consultation with governments. (n.d.). Retrieved from https://wwf.panda.org/discover/our_focus/wildlife_practice/problems/illegal_trade/wildlife_trade_campaign/wildlife_trafficking_report/

2. Beyond Wet Markets: The Many Problems With The Wildlife Trade. (2021). Retrieved 23 June 2021, from https://www.worldanimalprotection.us/blogs/wet-markets-problems-wildlife-trade

3. 7 Reasons We Need to End the Exotic Pet Trade. (2021). Retrieved 23 June 2021, from https://www.worldanimalprotection.us/blogs/exotic-pet-trade

4. Inside The Exotic Animal Trade | PETA. (2021). Retrieved 23 June 2021, from https://www.peta.org/issues/animal-companion-issues/animal-companion-factsheets/inside-exotic-animal-trade/

5. Exotic Animals as 'Pets' | PETA. (2021). Retrieved 23 June 2021, from https://www.peta.org/issues/animals-in-entertainment/exotic-animals-pets/

6. Souza, M. (2011). One Health: Zoonosis in the Exotic Animal Practice. Retrieved 23 June 2021, from https://www.ncbi.nlm.nih.gov/pmc/articles/PMC7110438/

7. Sheikh, P., & O'Regan, K. (2021). Wildlife Trade, COVID-19 and Other Zoonotic Diseases. Retrieved 23 April 2021, from https://crsreports.congress.gov/product/pdf/IF/IF11494

Bees

1. 10 facts about honey bees! (2020, September 16). Retrieved from https://www.natgeokids.com/za/discover/animals/insects/honey-bees/

2. Ethics, A. (2021). Exploitation of bees by humans - Animal Ethics. Retrieved 24 June 2021, from https://www.animal-ethics.org/exploitation-of-bees-by-humans/

3. Introduction. (n.d.). Retrieved from https://askabiologist.asu.edu/bee-dance-game/introduction.html

4. "Bumble Bees Can Estimate Time Intervals." ScienceDaily. ScienceDaily, 25 August 2006. <www.sciencedaily.com/releases/2006/08/060825103730.htm>.

5. The Role of the Queen Bee. (n.d.). Retrieved from https://www.perfectbee.com/learn-about-bees/the-life-of-bees/role-queen-bee

6. Bee Facts. (n.d.). Retrieved from https://honeybeenet.gsfc.nasa.gov/Honeybees/Basics.htm

7. Winters, E. (2020, July 19). Why don't vegans eat honey? Retrieved from https://www.youtube.com/watch?v=clMNw_VO1xo&ab_channel=EarthlingEd

8. Animal Cruelty - Honey. (2021). Retrieved 24 June 2021, from https://www.veganpeace.com/animal_cruelty/honey.htm

9. How many species of native bees are in the United States?. (2021). Retrieved 24 June 2021, from https://www.usgs.gov/faqs/how-many-species-native-bees-are-united-states?qt-news_science_products=0#qt-news_science_products

10. McGivney, A. (2021). 'Like sending bees to war': the deadly truth behind your almond milk obsession. Retrieved 24 June 2021, from https://www.theguardian.com/environment/2020/jan/07/honeybees-deaths-almonds-hives-aoe

11. Our Love Of Almonds Is Seriously Jeopardizing Honeybees. (2021). Retrieved 24 June 2021, from https://www.huffpost.com/entry/honey-bee-census-almonds_n_5d0a8726e4b0f7b7442b3aaa

12. 15 plants to help save bees. (2021). Retrieved 24 June 2021, from https://www.ecowatch.com/15-plants-to-help-save-bees-1881882632.html

13. What to Plant in Your Garden to Help Save the Bees. (2021). Retrieved 24 June 2021, from https://www.onegreenplanet.org/lifestyle/what-to-plant-in-your-garden-to-help-save-the-bees/

Silkworms

1. Ofei, M. Is Silk Vegan? The Answer Lies In The Process | The Minimalist Vegan. (2021). Retrieved 25 June 2021, from https://theminimalistvegan.com/is-silk-vegan/

2. Is Silk Vegan? For Every Pound, 3,000 Animals Are Killed | PETA. (2021). Retrieved from https://www.peta.org/blog/is-silk-vegan/

3. Silk Is Not Vegan — Learn How It's Made. (2021). Retrieved from https://www.treehugger.com/why-vegans-dont-wear-silk-127729

Humans

1. Imhoff, D., & Salatin, J. (2010). *CAFO (concentrated animal feeding operation): The tragedy of industrial animal factories.* Page 294. San Rafael, CA: Earth Aware.

2. Cannabis Laws & Penalties in Texas. (2021, March 12). Retrieved from https://www.texasnorml.org/activism/marijuana-laws-and-penalties-in-texas/

3. Tucker, W. (2018). The Kill Line. Retrieved 10 July 2021, from https://www.splcenter.org/news/2018/07/26/kill-line

4. *Meat Packing: Last Week Tonight With John Oliver* [Video file]. (2021, February 22). Retrieved from https://www.youtube.com/watch?v=IhO1FcjDMV4&ab_channel=LastWeekTonight

5. Stauffer, B. (2019, April). "When We're Dead and Buried, Our Bones Will Keep Hurting". Retrieved from https://www.hrw.org/report/2019/09/04/when-were-dead-and-buried-our-bones-will-keep-hurting/workers-rights-under-threat

6. Capps, A. (2020, March 25). Meat & Dairy Industries Prey On Vulnerable Humans and Nonhumans Alike. Retrieved from https://freefromharm.org/animal-products-and-ethics/slaughterhouses-prey-on-vulnerable-humans-and-animals/

7. Meatpacking and Slaughterhouses. (2021, March 17). Retrieved from https://foodprint.org/issues/meatpacking-and-slaughter-houses/

8. Imhoff, D. (2010). *CAFO (concentrated animal feeding operation): The tragedy of industrial animal factories.* Pages 37 & 45. San Rafael, CA: Earth Aware.

9. Compa, L. (2004). BLOOD, SWEAT & FEAR: Workers Rights in U.S. Meat and Poultry Packing Plants. Retrieved 10 July 2021, from https://www.hrw.org/reports/2005/usa0105/usa0105.pdf

10. Schlosser, E. & Imhoff, D. (2010). *CAFO (concentrated animal feeding operation): The tragedy of industrial animal factories.* Page 120. San Rafael, CA: Earth Aware.

11. Fishing among the most dangerous of all professions, says ILO. (1999, December 13). Retrieved from https://www.ilo.org/global/about-the-ilo/newsroom/news/WCMS_071324/lang--en/index.htm

12. Martini, R. (2019). Many government subsidies lead to overfishing. Here's a solution. Retrieved from https://www.oecd.org/agriculture/government-subsidies-overfishing/

13. UN appeals for $35 billion to help world's 'most vulnerable and fragile' in 2021 | | UN News. (2020). Retrieved from https://news.un.org/en/story/2020/12/1078852

14. FAO. (2006). Livestock's Long Shadow. Retrieved from https://www.fao.org/3/a0701e/a0701e.pdf

15. Imhoff, D., & Noble, M. (2010). *CAFO (concentrated animal feeding operation): The tragedy of industrial animal factories.* Page 130. San Rafael, CA: Earth Aware.

16. Freshwater, S. (2021). Understanding Emotions - Shawna Freshwater, PhD. Retrieved 22 September 2021, from https://spacious-therapy.com/understanding-emotions/

17. Hunt, T. (2021). The Hippies Were Right: It's All about Vibrations, Man!. Retrieved 22 September 2021, from https://blogs.scientificamerican.com/observations/the-hippies-were-right-its-all-about-vibrations-man/

Environmental Benefits of Veganism & Deficits of Carnism

1. Imhoff, D. (2010). *CAFO (concentrated animal feeding operation): The tragedy of industrial animal factories*. San Rafael, CA: Earth Aware.
2. The Sustainability Secret. (2014). Retrieved from https://www.cowspiracy.com/facts
3. United Nations. (2006). Rearing cattle produces more greenhouse gases than driving cars, UN report warns | | UN News. Retrieved from https://news.un.org/en/story/2006/11/201222-rearing-cattle-produces-more-greenhouse-gases-driving-cars-un-report-warns
4. Borunda, A. (2021, May 03). Methane facts and information. Retrieved from https://www.nationalgeographic.com/environment/article/methane?loggedin=true
5. Imhoff, D., Lappe, A., Noble, M. & (2010). *CAFO (concentrated animal feeding operation): The tragedy of industrial animal factories*. Pages 43, 131, 132, 135, 136, 238. San Rafael, CA: Earth Aware.
6. Harris, B., Shores, R., & Jones, L. (n.d.). AMMONIA EMISSION FACTORS FROM SWINE FINISHING OPERATIONS. Retrieved from https://www3.epa.gov/ttnchie1/conference/ei10/ammonia/harris.pdf
7. The Humane Society Of The United States. (n.d.). An HSUS Report: The Impact of Industrialized Animal Agriculture on the Environment. Retrieved from https://www.humanesociety.org/

sites/default/files/docs/hsus-report-industrialized-animal-agri-culture-environment.pdf

8. Konopacky, J. (2020). EWG Study and Mapping Show Big CAFOs in Iowa Up Fivefold Since 1990. Retrieved from https://www.ewg.org/interactive-maps/2020-iowa-cafos/

9. Imhoff, D., Tietz, J. (2010). *CAFO (concentrated animal feeding operation): The tragedy of industrial animal factories.* Pages 61-67. San Rafael, CA: Earth Aware.

10. Andersen, K., Kuhn, K., xTrue Naturex (Musical group),, A.U.M. Films & Media (Organization),, & First Spark Media,. (2014). *Cowspiracy: The sustainability secret.*

11. Total Water Use In The United States. (2015). Retrieved from https://www.usgs.gov/special-topic/water-science-school/science/total-water-use-united-states?qt-science_center_objects=0#qt-science_center_objects

12. Hallock, B. (2014, January 27). To make a burger, first you need 660 gallons of water ... Retrieved from https://www.latimes.com/food/dailydish/la-dd-gallons-of-water-to-make-a-burger-20140124-story.html

13. How much oxygen comes from the ocean? (n.d.). Retrieved from https://oceanservice.noaa.gov/facts/ocean-oxygen.html

14. FAO. (n.d.). General situation of world fish stocks. Retrieved from https://www.fao.org/Newsroom/common/ecg/1000505/en/stocks.pdf

15. Woody, T. (2021, May 03). The sea is running out of fish, despite nations' pledges to stop. Retrieved from https://www.nationalgeographic.com/science/article/sea-running-out-of-fish-despite-nations-pledges-to-stop?loggedin=true

16. Imhoff, D., Wuerthner, G. (2010). *CAFO (concentrated animal feeding operation): The tragedy of industrial animal factories.* Page 99. San Rafael, CA: Earth Aware.

17. Tickell, J. Kiss the Ground: How the Food You Eat Can Reverse Climate Change, Heal Your Body & Ultimately Save Our World (New York: Simon & Schuster, 2017)

18. WOLDEAB, R. (2019). How Industrialized Meat Production Causes Land Degradation. Retrieved 24 September 2021, from https://populationeducation.org/industrialized-meat-production-and-land-degradation-3-reasons-to-shift-to-a-plant-based-diet/

19. Cosier, S. (2019). The world needs topsoil to grow 95% of its food – but it's rapidly disappearing. Retrieved 24 September 2021, from https://www.theguardian.com/us-news/2019/may/30/topsoil-farming-agriculture-food-toxic-america

20. Harris, T. (2020, January 27). How Rainforests Work. Retrieved from https://science.howstuffworks.com/environmental/conservation/issues/rainforest5.htm

21. Unsustainable cattle ranching. (n.d.). Retrieved from https://wwf.panda.org/discover/knowledge_hub/where_we_work/amazon/amazon_threats/unsustainable_cattle_ranching/

22. Soy. (n.d.). Retrieved from https://wwf.panda.org/discover/our_focus/food_practice/sustainable_production/soy/

23. Animal Agriculture Is Destroying Tropical Forests. (2021). Retrieved from https://www.worldanimalfoundation.org/advocate/farm-animals/params/post/1280110/animal-agriculture-is-destroying-tropical-forests

24. Paranjpe, A. (2021). — United In Heart. Retrieved 24 September 2021, from https://unitedinheart.org/solutions/2021/1/31/our-strategy

25. Petter, O. (2020). Going vegan is 'single biggest way' to reduce our impact, study finds. Retrieved 24 September 2021, from https://www.independent.co.uk/life-style/health-and-families/veganism-environmental-impact-planet-reduced-plant-based-diet-humans-study-a8378631.html

Health Benefits of Veganism & Deficits of Carnism

1. Petre, A. (2021, May 19). 6 Science-Based Health Benefits of Eating Vegan. Retrieved from https://www.healthline.com/nutrition/vegan-diet-benefits#TOC_TITLE_HDR_3

2. Diabetes. (2021, April 13). Retrieved from https://www.who.int/news-room/fact-sheets/detail/diabetes

3. National Diabetes Statistics Report, 2020. (2020, February 11). Retrieved from https://www.cdc.gov/diabetes/library/features/diabetes-stat-report.html

4. What is diabetes? (2020, June 11). Retrieved from https://www.cdc.gov/diabetes/basics/diabetes.html

5. Editor. (2019, January 15). Milk and Diabetes. Retrieved from https://www.diabetes.co.uk/food/milk-and-diabetes.html

6. Sweeny, C. (2019, September 04). Following a healthy plant-based diet may lower type 2 diabetes risk. Retrieved from https://www.hsph.harvard.edu/news/press-releases/following-a-healthy-plant-based-diet-may-lower-type-2-diabetes-risk/

7. Davison, C. (2021, September 21). How a Vegan Diet Impacts Diabetes. Retrieved from https://www.forksoverknives.com/health-topics/vegan-diet-and-diabetes

8. Heart Disease Facts | cdc.gov. (2020). Retrieved from https://www.cdc.gov/heartdisease/facts.htm

9. What is Cardiovascular Disease? (n.d.). Retrieved from https://www.heart.org/en/health-topics/consumer-healthcare/what-is-cardiovascular-disease

10. Campbell, T. and Campbell, T., 2004. *The China study: The Most Comprehensive Study Of Nutrition Ever Conducted.* Pgs.5, 12, 14, 111-131, 159-163

11. *New Review Highlights Benefits of Plant-Based Diets for Heart Health.* Physicians Committee for Responsible Medicine. (2018). Retrieved 6 October 2021, from https://www.pcrm.org/news/news-releases/new-review-highlights-benefits-plant-based-diets-heart-health.

12. Madigan M, Karhu E. The role of plant-based nutrition in cancer prevention. *J Unexplored Med Data* 2018;3:9. https://jumdjournal.net/article/view/2892

13. Staff. (2015). WHO report says eating processed meat is carcinogenic: Understanding the findings. Retrieved from https://www.hsph.harvard.edu/nutritionsource/2015/11/03/report-says-eating-processed-meat-is-carcinogenic-understanding-the-findings/

14. American Cancer Society. *Cancer Facts & Figures 2006.* Atlanta, GA: American Cancer Society; 2006. http://www.cancer.org/acs/groups/content/@nho/documents/document/caff2006pwsecuredpdf.pdf

15. Christen, C. (2021, September 08). Meat Consumption in the U.S. Is Growing at an Alarming Rate. Retrieved from https://sentientmedia.org/meat-consumption-in-the-us/

16. Physicians Committee for Responsible Medicine. n.d. *Health Concerns About Dairy.* [online] Available at: <https://www.pcrm.org/

good-nutrition/nutrition-information/health-concerns-about-dairy>

Foods To Consume For Healthy Vegan Living

1. Moore, M., 2014. *Leafy Greens: Nutrition Rock Stars - Food & Nutrition Magazine.* [online] Food & Nutrition Magazine. Available at: <https://foodandnutrition.org/march-april-2014/leafy-greens-nutrition-rock-stars/>
2. Medicalnewstoday.com. n.d. *15 healthiest vegetables: Nutrition and health benefits.* [online] Available at: <https://www.medicalnewstoday.com/articles/323319#13.-Bell-peppers>
3. Healthline. n.d. *20 Tasty Fruits with Health Benefits.* [online] Available at: <https://www.healthline.com/nutrition/healthy-fruit>
4. Zelman, K., 2011. *Tips for Reaping the Benefits of Whole Grains.* [online] WebMD. Available at: <https://www.webmd.com/food-recipes/features/reap-the-benefits-of-whole-grains#3>
5. Medlineplus.gov. n.d. *Healthy food trends - beans and legumes: MedlinePlus Medical Encyclopedia.* [online] Available at: <https://medlineplus.gov/ency/patientinstructions/000726.htm>
6. Harvard Health. 2017. *Why nutritionists are crazy about nuts - Harvard Health.* [online] Available at: <https://www.health.harvard.edu/nutrition/why-nutritionists-are-crazy-about-nuts>
7. Healthline. n.d. *8 Health Benefits of Eating Nuts.* [online] Available at: <https://www.healthline.com/nutrition/8-benefits-of-nuts#TOC_TITLE_HDR_10>
8. Cleveland Clinic. 2021. *The 6 Best Seeds to Eat.* [online] Available at: <https://health.clevelandclinic.org/the-6-best-seeds-to-eat/>

9. Capps, A. (2018, January 15). B12: A Magic Pill, or Veganism's Achilles Heel? Retrieved from https://freefromharm.org/health-nutrition/b12-magic-pill-veganisms-achilles-heel/

10. Psihoyos, L., Chan, J., Cameron, J., Schwarzenegger, A. The Game Changers. (2019, October 16). Retrieved from https://www.net-flix.com/title/81157840

11. McGrane, K. (2020, April 21). 13 Nearly Complete Protein Sources for Vegetarians and Vegans. Retrieved from https://www.healthline.com/nutrition/complete-protein-for-ve-gans#11.-Pita-and-hummus

Acknowledgments

Thank you to my blessing of a mother, Tina, for bringing me into this world and always encouraging me to be compassionate, generous and true to myself. Thank you to my incredible partner, Justin, for loving me wholly and supporting me completely. Thank you to you both for the hours you've poured into this book and the edits, comments and thoughts you've contributed. I'm so grateful to have you two on my team. I love you dearly.

Thank you to my amazing friends, whom I consider my family. You've given me what I've always yearned for: community. Thank you to those who volunteered at Plant and who supported it in any way. The people of Plant were always wonderful and it's because of you that my memories of that era are filled with love, laughter and joy. Thank you especially to Koda, for being the bright bubble of sunshine that you are and for your feedback and support on this book. And thank you Carolyna, for being the powerful, confident woman you are and encouraging me to to live to my fullest potential.

Thank you to everyone I have ever done activism with. Thank you to everyone who is involved in activism. Thank you for being vocal for justice. Thank you for standing for peace.

Thank you for choosing compassionate action. Thank you, especially Jocelyn, for being an inspiring first impression of what an activist is.

Thank you to the creators of What The Health & Earthlings, for motivating me to go vegan and changing my life forever.

Thank you to the animals whom I have met and those I have not. Thank you to Buddy for showing me what it feels like to truly bond with a cow. Thank you to literally every goat I've ever met. I freaking love you all. Thank you to the pigs Ironman & Archie for being yourselves. Thank you for rolling over and allowing me to rub your bellies. Thank you to those I locked eyes with in the factory farms. You radicalized me in a way that has led to the creation of this book, which I dearly hope will help the situation of your kind.

Thank you to everyone who has rescued animals. Thank you to everyone who is vegan. Thank you to everyone who is reading these words. Thank you for being open, receptive and willing to listen, contemplate and grow.

Thank you for being here now.